BRIGHT NOTES

SLAUGHTERHOUSE-FIVE BY KURT VONNEGUT

Intelligent Education

Nashville, Tennessee

BRIGHT NOTES: Slaughterhouse-Five
www.BrightNotes.com

ISBN: 978-1-645423-02-7 (Paperback)
ISBN: 978-1-645423-03-4 (eBook)

Published in accordance with the U.S. Copyright Office Orphan Works and Mass Digitization report of the register of copyrights, June 2015.

Originally published by Monarch Press.
Walter James Miller; Bonnie E. Nelson, 1973
2019 Edition published by Influence Publishers.

Interior design by Lapiz Digital Services. Cover Design by Thinkpen Designs.

Printed in the United States of America.

Library of Congress Cataloging-in-Publication Data forthcoming.
Names: Intelligent Education
Title: BRIGHT NOTES: Slaughterhouse-Five
Subject: STU004000 STUDY AIDS / Book Notes

CONTENTS

INTRODUCTION TO KURT VONNEGUT

VONNEGUT'S LIFE, WORKS, AND CRITICAL REPUTATION

For twenty years, Kurt Vonnegut found it hard to get going on his anti-war novel. Then he saw the way to do it. He realized that his troubles in facing the story were an essential part of the story. So he wrote *Slaughterhouse-Five* as a double story: the main character suffers from the traumatic effects of war; the author struggles with the effects of war on both the character and the author. Neat. Vonnegut sees that under certain circumstances, we simply must view a work of art with the author in mind. He had been moving toward this conviction all through the Sixties. In public appearances, he found audiences just naturally accepting the idea. Student audiences especially are happy to junk the old distinction between Creation and Creator. He answered their questions, illustrated his notions, with abundant detail from his personal life. Preparing a new edition of *Mother Night*, he added a preface about his personal experiences with Nazism. He prologued *Welcome to the Monkey House* by relating his main **themes** to his brother, sister, wife. His new approach made it easy for him to finish *Slaughterhouse-Five*. And by the time he was writing an introduction to *Happy Birthday, Wanda June*, he was committed to the confessional mode. Art is no longer a finished product - it is an ongoing process. Obviously there are limits to how intimate Vonnegut feels an artist has to be. But this much is certain. He wants us to see that his basic life story is one work that sheds light on all his other works.

VONNEGUT'S EARLY LIFE

Family Background And Influence

Kurt Vonnegut, Jr., was ironic even on the day of his birth. He arrived in Indianapolis, Indiana, on November 11, 1922, a day then celebrated as "Armistice Day," now called "Veterans Day," and a day destined to figure in Vonnegut's fiction. Kurt Junior was the third child born to Kurt Senior and Edith Sophia Lieber Vonnegut. Kurt Senior was a third-generation German-American, son of an architect, and himself an architect. He also painted. A physically frail man, he apparently sought compensation for his frailty by collecting guns and hunting. During the Great Depression, Kurt Senior went for eleven years without one architectural commission: but he was sufficiently well-off so his family of five did not suffer materially. Mrs. Vonnegut was active in the cultural and intellectual life of the area. Her father owned the brewery that made Lieber Lager, a beer that won the Gold Medal at the Paris **Exposition**. According to Vonnegut the author, the secret ingredient in Lieber Lager was coffee.

In a day characterized by a growing "generation gap," the older Vonneguts enjoyed a creative relationship with their children. Perhaps they merited it because they were forward-looking. They were skeptical, liberal, pacifistic in their attitudes, cautious about all generalizations and systems of thought. The Vonnegut household entertained painters, sculptors, intellectuals. Kurt Senior was a passionate believer in the positive values of technology, and he encouraged his children to be scientific in their interests, or at least utilitarian.

Mrs. Vonnegut succeeded in teaching the children how to be grammatical in a graceful way. The children were free to express their differences with their parents. Once Kurt Senior shot a quail. The oldest child, Bernard - eight years older than Kurt Junior - looked at the dead bird and said, "My gosh, that's like smashing a fine Swiss watch." And Alice, five years older than Kurt Junior, cried and refused to eat when her father brought home game. The reactions of Kurt Junior are clear in his later work: to him, Odysseus is neither a hero nor a villain. And when a Life reporter once asked him where he got his "youth-minded notions," the author of *Slaughterhouse-Five* said "I got them from my parents. I thought about it and decided they were right."

Brother Bernard became a physicist. He took his bachelor's and doctor's degrees at Massachusetts Institute of Technology, became a professor of atmospheric sciences in the State University of New York, fathered five sons, and made Who's Who well ahead of his brother. Sister Alice became a sculptor; she died at the age of forty leaving her three sons to her younger brother. Kurt Junior has acknowledged in his writing the way siblings Bernard, Alice, and Kurt Junior have all agreed in spirit.

Youth And Education

Kurt Junior from the beginning combined the esthetic with the technical. He remembers reading Edgar Lee Masters' *Spoon-River Anthology* when he was twelve and realizing "all those people had to be what they were." In Shortridge High School, he became editor of the daily paper, the *Echo*. In Indianapolis, he recalls, there were some "vile and lively native American fascists." Somebody slipped him a copy of *The Protocols of the Elders of Zion*, a fictitious work purporting to be the secrets plans of the Jews for taking over the world. It was equally written by a notorious anti-Semite and had become part of the secret plans of the Nazis for taking over the world. Vonnegut recalls too how one of his aunts married "a German" and had to write back to Indianapolis for proof that she had "no Jewish blood." The mayor had known her from high school and dancing school. "He had fun," Vonnegut says, "putting ribbons and official seals all over the documents the Germans required, which made them look like eighteenth-century peace treaties." Most Americans still tended to regard Hitler and Mussolini as comic-opera characters.

Expected to become a scientist, Vonnegut chose to major in biochemistry when he entered Cornell University in 1940. "Chemistry," he recalls, "was a magic word in the thirties. The Germans ... had chemistry, and they were going to take apart the universe and put it back together again." In 1942 Vonnegut became editor of the *Cornell Sun*. He later transferred to Carnegie Institute of Technology and was in his junior year when he was inducted into the army.

Military Service

Private Vonnegut took his basic training in Artillery but was later transferred to the Infantry as a battalion scout. He went into combat during the Battle of the Bulge, when the Nazi armies broke through the Allied lines in a powerful last bid for victory. For what he believes to have been eleven days straight, Private Vonnegut was cut off from his unit and wandered around in Luxembourg inside the German lines. There he was captured. Under the terms of the Geneva **Convention**, he had to work for his keep. He was assigned to a group of one-hundred American prisoners who were sent to Dresden. They were "put out as contract labor," Vonnegut says, "to a factory that was making a vitamin-enriched malt syrup for pregnant women." The syrup, which has figured literally and symbolically in Vonnegut's work, "tasted like thin honey laced with hickory smoke." Dresden was then the most beautiful "baroque" city in Europe, still unscathed by war: there were no troop concentrations there, no war industries, no military targets. It was considered, under international law, to be an "open city," not to be attacked.

Dresden Versus Auschwitz

But on the night of February 13, 1945, American and British planes dropped high explosives on Dresden. There were no specific targets, just the general plan that bombs would drive firemen off the streets. Then hundreds of thousands of incendiary torpedoes were loosed on the city. More planes dropped explosives to discourage firemen. All the separate fires joined to become one holocaust: a fire-storm, the greatest massacre in history, the greatest single atrocity of all time: 135,000 civilians in an open city dead by morning. Vonnegut did not see the fire-storm. He could only hear it and feel it. He, his 99 fellow Americans and six German guards were in a deep underground meat-locker beneath Schlachthof-Funf, Slaughterhouse-five, the 100 prisoners' barrack. When they emerged, the malt-syrup factory was gone, everything - cathedrals, museums, parks, the zoo - everything and everybody was gone. The American prisoners were put to work as "corpse miners," as Vonnegut describes it, "breaking into shelters, bringing bodies out."

Asked later how he felt about the Dresden fire-raid, he said, "The burning ... was in response to the savagery of the Nazis, and fair really was fair, except that it gets confusing when you see the victims ... what we had seen cleaning out the shelters was as fancy as what we would have seen cleaning out the crematoria. How do you balance off Dresden against Auschwitz? Do you balance it off; or is it all so absurd it's silly to talk about it?" And later as a civilian, he wrote to the Air Force asking for information about the Dresden raid; a public relations man wrote back that the raid was still "top secret."

YEARS OF TRANSITION: 1945–1950

After "V-E" Day, Vonnegut's work-group was rescued by the Russians. They were exchanged, man-for-man, for Russian prisoners-of-war rescued by the Americans. They were sent to a rest camp, and then back to the States. Vonnegut was decorated with the Purple Heart. By late summer of 1945 he was courting Jane Marie Cox. They had known each other since they attended kindergarten together. But while he went to Cornell, Carnegie, and combat, she went to Swarthmore, where she made Phi Beta Kappa. A summer afternoon they enjoyed together provided Vonnegut with material for a story he was to write years later: "Long Walk to Forever." They were married on September 1, 1945. A few weeks later Kurt Vonnegut entered the University of Chicago under the GI Bill. Here he majored in anthropology. To his studies in this area her partly attributes his feeling that "all men are the same and ... there are no villains." In 1946 he supplemented his GI educational allotment by working as a police reporter for the Chicago City News Bureau. The first story he covered provided him with a bizarre instance of accidental death caused by machinery, which was to figure in *Slaughterhouse-Five* along with his wartime experiences. In 1947 he dropped out of school without a degree to take a full-time job as a public-relations writer with General Electric in Schenectady, New York. The Vonneguts bought a house in Alplaus, where he became a volunteer fireman: badge 155. (Later, in *God Bless You, Mr. Rosewater*, he would define a "press agent" as "an ultimately dishonest man" and say that Rosewater was serving as a volunteer fireman to placate his conscience for having killed German firemen in World War II.) Vonnegut started to write, nights and weekends, because he hated his job at GE: he was confident he could "write himself out of it." From the beginning, he had the Dresden fire-storm in mind as the big story that he had to write. But somehow he kept postponing that, not always sure why. Instead he took up some science-fiction **themes** which came more easily at the moment: he had a good background in science and technology. He sold his first novel, *Player Piano*, and left GE for good in 1950. He really had to now, for *Player Piano* is partly a **satire** on General Electric (which becomes General Forge and Foundry) and on Schenectady (which becomes Ilium, New York). The world of the future envisioned in *Player Piano* is run by computers. Only those human beings who can compete economically with computers - only those whose "I.Q.'s" are high or whose occupations are not yet automated - have any dignity or freedom in this new world. The rest of the population are reduced to uselessness, humiliated and ready for revolution. But even some managers (one of them unwittingly demotes himself by inventing machinery that can do his job!) turn against the system. The hero, Paul Proteus, becomes disillusioned with violent revolution as well as with repressive management. Some of the best scenes are those in which Paul learns the extent to which the corporation spies on its employees and brainwashes even the company wives.

FREE-LANCE WRITING: THE FIFTIES

Short Stories

Vonnegut claims to have learned the writer's craft from manuals on magazine writing. Wilfred Sheed suggests we take this with a grain of salt, but Vonnegut's short stories of this period speak for themselves. Vonnegut had to make a living selling to the big "commercial" magazines. In those days that meant writing very close to a rigid formula: narration had to be "linear"; conflict had to be dramatized in scenes with dialogue, "rising action" had to quickly overcome "**exposition**" (background explanation), there had to be a "**climax**" with swift "falling action" and of course a "healthful" ending that avoided taboos (of divorce, despair, and other unpleasantness). Vonnegut learned this trade well: in his career as a "slick" story writer he sold more than 100 stories to such top magazines as *Saturday Evening Post, McCall's, Cosmopolitan, Ladies' Home Journal, Colliers, Galaxy, Fantasy and Science Fiction*. Most of these "slick" pieces are ingenious in conception but necessarily conventional in treatment. "During most of my freelancing," Vonnegut told C. D. B. Bryan, "I made what I would have made in charge of the cafeteria at a ... good junior high school." And in his preface to his collection of these stories, he refers to them as "samples of work I sold in order to finance the writing of the novels. Here one finds the fruits of Free Enterprise." Vonnegut's identification with the "slicks" apparently prejudiced most critics against his early novels. They barely noticed *Player Piano* (1952) and it sold only 3500 copies in its first edition. For years it was known mainly to devotees of science fiction, although it deserved to be reviewed at least as a serious novel of social criticism.

Odd Jobs

Given the generous share-the-wealth policy of American magazine publishers (whose "slicks" and "pulps" reached millions of homes and made fortunes for their owners), it is no wonder Vonnegut had to supplement his earnings as a writer with various odd jobs. The Vonneguts were paying off a mortgage on a rambling farmhouse in west Barnstable on Cape Cod, Massachusetts, Vonnegut became the first Saab dealer in the United States and took a $1000 commission for a large piece of decorative sculpture for a motel at Logan Airport, Boston. Vonnegut only designed the work, sub-contracting the actual rendering to a Cape Cod welder. This work stood in the motel lobby until late in the Sixties.

Six Children

By now the Vonnegut's were bringing up three children of their own: Mark, Edith, and Nanette. In 1957, Vonnegut's sister Alice died and the author adopted her three boys: James, Steven, and Kurt Adams. (The two girls will figure a decade later in the river-crossing trip to Philadelphia in chapter 1 of *Slaughterhouse-Five*; the four boys are the original audience for the author's views on massacres and massacre-machinery expressed in the same chapter.)

"Natural Childbirth"

One night at a party, a publishing-house editor asked Vonnegut, "Why don't you write another book?"

Vonnegut replied, "Well, I have an idea for one."

"Tell me about it," the editor urged, and they went into a bedroom. Actually Vonnegut had not formulated anything definite, but he just started talking and out came the story for *The Sirens of Titan*.

"Every mother's favorite child," Vonnegut says, "is the one that's delivered by natural childbirth. The Sirens of Titan was that kind of book." He calls it the only book that was "pleasant to write." This experience provides the basis for that scene in *Slaughterhouse-Five* in which Kilgore Trout is asked, "What's the most famous thing you ever wrote?" Off the top of his head, while eating canapés of salmon roe and cream cheese, Trout spins a yarn about a "great French chef," making it up as he goes along.

During this same period, Vonnegut began experimenting with plays. His *Something Borrowed* was produced in summer stock in 1958. The *Sirens of Titan* was published in 1959. The action takes place on Earth, Mars, and Mercury, and on a remote mythical planet called Tralfamadore. Extraterrestrial forces arrange the entire course of human history to provide an intergalactic messenger with a spare part for his space ship! The novel draws on the whole range of Vonnegut's thinking and experience: it satirizes American advertising, the corporation mentality, the military mind; it makes effective **allusions** to painters and it shows that its author knows how it feels to clean a rifle and live in a barrack. The Sirens of Titan is an early expression of Vonnegut's belief that any pattern of reality might actually be controlled by a larger pattern outside itself. (Tralfamadore, the home planet of the intergalactic messenger, later will reappear briefly in *God Bless You, Mr. Rosewater* and will figure significantly in *Slaughterhouse-Five*.)

SUCCESS IN THE SIXTIES

Vonnegut On Homer And Hemingway

In 1960, life on Cape Cod seemed "boring" and the Vonneguts decided to take a Great Books course. They re-read Homer's

Odyssey. As Vonnegut recalls it: "Odysseus' coming home from the war really got to me. His behavior struck me as cruel.... The hero-warrior ... seemed so preposterous in modern times.... I felt free to imagine a modern Odysseus ... a lot like that part of Hemingway which I detested - the slayer of nearly extinct animals which meant him harm no.... I didn't like that. So I sat down and wrote a play because I wanted to try my hand at another form." *Penelope*, as it was called, was tried out experimentally for one week at the Orleans Arena Theatre on Cape Cod. Then, Vonnegut says, he "threw the manuscript into an empty beer carton along with two other plays." He returned to his fiction. Later a producer talked him into doing another version of Penelope. "The original germ - about our need for heroes and our fear of death - remains," Vonnegut said. "But now it's about a new kind of American hero - the hero who refuses to kill." This version became the basis of the rewritten play ultimately to run in New York as *Happy Birthday, Wanda June*.

Two Books In 1961

He would be continually tempted into the theatre from now on. He was active in the Barnstable amateur theater group and one of his best stories of this period, "What Am I This Time?" (1961), shows how drama was making him question the relation between art and life. Still, it was in fiction that he made his mark in the Sixties. In 1961, he published his first collection of short stories, *Canary in a Cathouse*, and his third novel, *Mother Night*. The former represents the kind of conventional fiction he was trying to leave behind; the latter represents the new, experimental Vonnegut. *Mother Night* is about the evil ironies of our time: its main character, Howard W. Campbell, Jr., is an American writer married to a German woman. At the outbreak of World War II, he stays in Germany ostensibly to serve as a radio propagandist for the Nazis. Secretly he's an American agent: his broadcasts contain coded information for Washington. It later becomes clear that Campbell has done more for the Nazis in his public role than he has done for the Americans in his secret role. The novel is told in a radically new way: in short segmented bursts. Some chapters are less than one page long. (Campbell, in his public role, will appear again in *Slaughterhouse-Five.*) The entire story of *Mother Night* draws heavily on Vonnegut's impressions and experience in the mid-West during the Thirties, when American Nazis were rampant in Indianapolis and his own aunt encountered the new race laws of the German Germans. Mother Night developed a large following for Vonnegut in the Bohemias (Greenwich Village, San Francisco) and on campus.

Turning Point: "Cat's Cradle"

But the novel that really established Vonnegut's reputation appeared in 1963. *Cat's Cradle* is an off-beat science-versus-religion story. It begins as a probe of the way the fathers of the atomic bomb behaved on the day Hiroshima was destroyed; its main action continues on an imaginary island in the Caribbean; there descendants of one inventor of the Bomb release the force that locks Earth in an icy death. Written in a first-person, impressionistic, segmented style that would serve Vonnegut well in writing *Slaughterhouse-Five, Cat's Cradle* provided the now-growing Vonnegut cult with an entire mythology and vocabulary. The novel is a parable spun from a philosophy called Bokononism, replete with scripture and terms like: karass, the sum total of your genuine, meaningful personal relationships; granfalloon, a false karass, an artificial association, such as your graduating class or the staff at GE; and foma, salutary illusions. The chief Bokononist doctrine is that karasses are to be taken seriously and granfalloons are not, while you "live by the foma that make you brave, kind, and happy." Vonnegut claims that he picked up the term karass off the name-plate of a Cape Cod mailbox! Graham Greene, the British novelist (*Brighton Rock, The Power and the Glory, The Third Man*), called *Cat's Cradle* "one of the three best novels of the year by one of the most able living writers."

Drama And Fiction

Two more of Vonnegut's plays were produced in summer stock while he was working on his fifth novel. The play *EPICAC* (1963) is based on one of Vonnegut's very early short stories by the same name (1950). It's about a computer which/who helps a male programmer with his courtship of a female programmer. But the computer itself/himself falls in love with the same lady and, frustrated, short-circuits itself to death. *EPICAC* appears also in *The Player Piano*. The whole concept is an interesting play with cybernetics and foreshadows the dilemma of HAL in the A. C. Clarke novel, 2001. In 1964 another Vonnegut play, *My Name Is Everyone*, was produced on Cape Cod, and one year later *God Bless You, Mr. Rosewater* was published. Set in Vonnegut's Indiana, this novel features a type of character that fascinates Vonnegut: the man of inherited wealth rich enough to perform any experiment. Eliot Rosewater (whose name connotes that of several of "America's Sixty Families" and also suggests a cologne used to mask odors) sets up a Foundation to help those people who have been deprived of their purpose (usefulness) in life through no fault of their own. Resorting more and more now to bursts of straight **exposition** alternating with dramatized scenes, Vonnegut satirizes the way the rich use religion, the mythology of the "work ethic," and constitutional government to keep themselves in power. Eliot is considered a traitor to his class, and "insane" because of his belief that people need all the uncritical love they can get. This eccentric philanthropist shares some (non-economic) experiences with Vonnegut himself: Rosewater has awful visions of Dresden; he is a compulsive volunteer-fireman by way of atonement for the killing of German firemen in World War II. Among the novel's famous passages is Rosewater's impromptu speech to a **convention** of science-fiction writers, praising them as the only ones "crazy enough" to contemplate what's really happening to mankind. The mythical "sci-fi" writer Kilgore Trout appears in this novel, significantly, as the **deus ex machina** who saves the situation. (Later we shall note the parallels to *Slaughterhouse-Five*, in which Rosewater brings the good word about "sci-fi" to Billy Pilgrim who in turn is brought closer to his own experience by the very presence of Kilgore Trout.) *God Bless You, Mr. Rosewater* convinced Vonnegut enthusiasts that he was on his way toward a magnum opus, but New Yorker magazine saw the style as "a series of narcissistic giggles."

Vonnegut Lectures At Iowa

For years a favorite among undergraduates, Vonnegut now gained recognition by the professors. In 1965 he was invited for a two-year stint as lecturer in the famous University of Iowa Writers Workshop. Meanwhile his growing popularity justified re-issue of two novels: *Player Piano* (1952) was long out of print and *Mother Night* (1961) had originally been issued only in paperback. In Iowa City, 1966, Vonnegut wrote his "Introduction" to the new hardcover edition of *Mother Night* in which he gave his first full-length description of his experiences at Dresden, recalled his brush with native fascists in Indianapolis in the Thirties, and made his now-famous comment on his hapless main character, Howard Campbell: "this is the only story of mine whose moral I know... . We are what we pretend to be, so we must be careful about what we pretend to be." This insight is prefigured in Vonnegut's story, "What Am I This Time?" and apparently stemmed from his theatrical experience. During his second year at Iowa, Vonnegut wrote an offbeat, impressionistic review of the *Random House Dictionary* for the *New York Times.* Gently he ridiculed the academicians' awesome distinctions between "prescriptive" and "descriptive" lexicographers and recalled the common sense his mother used in teaching him to say, "Am I not?" This piece was later included in *Welcome to the Monkey House.*

First Serious Critical Attention

While he was at Iowa, Vonnegut received his first serious critical attention. Until 1966, most Establishment critics had either ignored him or tacitly disparaged him. They tended to view *Player Piano* and *The Sirens of Titan* as mere science fiction, outside the realm of belles lettres. They apparently overlooked the original edition of *Mother Night* because in those days, any work appearing only in paperback was beneath consideration. Things looked better for Vonnegut when Graham Greene praised *Cat's Cradle* and when a small group of other established authors, like Conrad Aiken and Nelson Algren, and "underground" writers like Terry Southern and Jules Feiffer, confessed to being Vonnegut fans. But when *God Bless You, Mr. Rosewater* (1965) appeared, most critics still would not admit Vonnegut to full literary recognition-now he was labeled as a "black humorist" or a "cult writer." But re-issue in 1966 of *Player Piano* and *Mother Night* provided Richard Schickel, author and critic, with the occasion for making a "historical appraisal in the hopes that it will encourage serious people to take Vonnegut seriously." In a full-length article in Harper's, Schickel proposed to demonstrate that "from the start of his career to the present,

Vonnegut has been a man with a unique vision seeking and finally finding the most effective manner of stating it."

Vonnegut's vision, according to Schickel, is that:

> ... all ideologies, all elaborate programs for mass progress, whether technological, political, or sociological, are frauds men perpetrate on themselves. The best the individual can do is try to protect himself from their broad sweepings and perhaps by remaining true to himself (even if this involves lonely martyrdom) bear witness against them. Vonnegut is that kind of rationalist who even suspects rationalism when it is converted into a program of belief.

To demonstrate how Vonnegut's vision remains constant while his strategies change, Schickel reviews the conflicts of the main characters in *Player Piano* and *Mother Night*. The difference between Proteus and Campbell, he concludes, is one of degree. "Campbell has moved beyond revolutionary illusion and is attempting to protect his secret, sacred self. But even such a limited program has joined revolution on Vonnegut's list of impossibilities," and Campbell's fate is essentially the same as Proteus'. Schickel sees this "narrowing of the individual's limits" as accounting for Vonnegut's new style. In *Player Piano,* he is still concerned with "realistic detailing," "believable plotting," "rounded characterization." But in *Mother Night*, Vonnegut now sees our world as so weird that anything may be allowed to happen "without explanation and without straining credulity." As a result, *Mother Night* is a "short, intensely charged book, its chapters are quick, deft sketches, almost revue blackouts ... a marvelously compressed piece of writing." Like *Cat's Cradle* and *God Bless You, Mr. Rosewater*, "*Mother Night* is a wonderful splash of bright, primary colors, an artful zestful cartoon that lets us see despair without forcing us to surrender to it." Schickel concludes that over the years "Vonnegut has advanced from diagnostician to exorcist, finding in intensified comic art the magic analgesic for ... temporary relief of existential pain."

First Serious Scholarly Attention

In 1967, Robert Scholes, the critic whose *New York Times* review of Barth's *Giles-Goatboy* had greatly enhanced Barth's reputation - published his scholarly study, *The Fabulators*. For the first time, Vonnegut was treated seriously as a writer in the mainstream of belles lettres. Scholes argues for the values of the new non-realistic fiction and includes Vonnegut among such great company as Lawrence Durrell and John Barth. Describing Vonnegut as an inheritor of both the "picaresque" and "satiric" traditions, Scholes demonstrates how and why Vonnegut departs from conventional **satire**. Scholes offers good definitions of **Black Humor** and makes neat distinctions between the answer offered by the Black Humorist and that offered by existentialism.

"Work In Progress"

A reference book in 1967 described Vonnegut as "adapting *Cat's Cradle* for Broadway production" and listed *Slaughterhouse-Five* as a "work in progress." This was the year that Vonnegut accepted a Guggenheim Fellowship to complete his novel about his war experiences. He used the money to go back to Dresden and also traveled to Hamburg, Vienna, Salzburg, Leningrad and Helsinki. With additional financial backing from his editor Seymour Lawrence, Vonnegut was now in his final confrontation with the incomprehensible memories of the Dresden fire-raid.

Autobiographical Preface

In 1968 he published his collection of twenty-five short stories and essays, *Welcome to the Monkey House*, and prefaced it with a brief but poignant statement of the relationship of his **themes** to his family life. He recalls his brother Bernard as writing about his first experience as a father: "Here I am cleaning shit off practically everything." He recalls his sister's dying words: "No pain." And he suggests now that the "two main themes" of his novels have already been succinctly stated by his siblings. In this essay Vonnegut extends his free-associational, impressionistic, "alogical" style to his nonfiction. The manner of the preface stands in strong contrast to the manner of most of the more conventionally treated pieces that follow.

On The Lecture Circuit

Meanwhile Vonnegut was alternating his writing with frequent public appearances. In 1968 he lectured at the Sophomore Literary Festival at Notre Dame. Granville Hicks described him as a "mild mannered man, respectable and even genteel in appearance," who got away "with a series of hilarious and subversive remarks on life and literature." The students, according to Hicks, had previously thought of Vonnegut as a science-fiction writer and now "came to realize how much more than that he is." And in February 1969, on the very eve of publication of his masterpiece, Vonnegut addressed the annual **convention** of the American Association of Physics teachers. His topic was "The Virtuous Physicist." Vonnegut defined him as the physicist who refuses to work on weapons. In an oblique reference to the growing domination of science by the military, he added that "some physicists are so virtuous that they're not going into physics."

Slaughterhouse-Five: A Critical Success

Finally, in late March, 1969, Vonnegut published his long awaited war novel. Its subject is the traumatic effect of the Dresden raid on both the main character and the narrator. For the narrator, the story has taken 23 years of procrastination: how can you write anything intelligent about a massacre? For the main character, Billy Pilgrim, the war has resulted in almost life-long stultification, quiet conformity in public life, escapist fantasy in private life. And the entire story - narrator's and main character's - is told in segmented images, with few overt transitions, and with sweeps back and forth across time.

Slaughterhouse-Five was an instant success. There were 20,000 advance sales, the book was named a Literary Guild alternate selection, it was optioned to the movies. The popular media hailed it with unusual unanimity. Robert Scholes wrote a front-page essay for the *New York Times Book Review*, C. D. B. Bryan wrote an "inside" story briefing those who had never heard of Vonnegut, Wilfrid Sheed devoted a whole page to the novel in *Life, Time* magazine gave it the lead review. Even those critics and periodicals that had previously taken a dim view of Vonnegut's work were forced now to devote space to him, even if just to explain why they disapproved of him. Vonnegut's sudden national popularity called for re-issue of all five earlier novels. This set off a second big wave of criticism, as major critics like Benjamin DeMott seized the occasion to evaluate Vonnegut's complete output. For the first time, the first five novels were widely discussed in the national media, both for their individual merit and as precursors of *Slaughterhouse-Five*.

A full discussion of these "two successive waves of criticism" will be found in the chapter "Critics Respond to *Slaughterhouse-Five*." An in-depth study of the novel itself will be found in chapters headed: " **Themes** and Techniques," "Textual Analysis" and "Characterization."

Public Image: The Vonneguts of Barnstable

Vonnegut has always held audiences with a kind of bardic magnetism. Now journalists tried to explain his personal charm and found themselves drawn into using Vonnegutian **metaphor**. Bryan described Vonnegut's brow as "chevroned like a sergeant-major's sleeve" and compared the author's green eyes to those of a "sacrificial altar-bound virgin caught in mid-shrug." Sheed wrote that Vonnegut walks in "a diffident bloodhound lope" and laughs with "a wild glee that stops just this side of a coughing fit." Estimates of Vonnegut's height ranged up to six-feet-three, his weight over 200, the first figure an exaggeration of only one inch, the second naturally variable. Writers commented on the fact that Vonnegut prefers to play his politics by ear ("He won't be trussed up in an ism, even a good one," Sheed said) but noted that he acknowledges membership in the Unitarian Church. Vonnegut's personal views on the Vietnam War were widely aired and doubtless contributed to the growing anti-war sentiment. Vonnegut declared flatly that he had four boys who were not going into the military. One was reported as living in a commune in British Columbia, another in Jamaica. Life magazine featured pictures of the Vonneguts in their Barnstable home: a two-story, clapboard-and-shingle farmhouse. Mrs. Vonnegut was photographed trimming his hair for "a night at the theatre." One reporter gave the text of a sign he had seen on the wall: "God damn it, you've got to be kind." The reporter apparently did not know that this is one of Eliot Rosewater's expostulations.

SELF-REVALUATION: THE SEVENTIES

Vonnegut's Right And Left Hands

1970 was in some respects Vonnegut's best year, and certainly a year of profound self-revaluation. He had seven books (six novels and a collection of short pieces) in print in both hardcover and paperback, he finally reached the theatre capital with a full-length play, and he taught at Harvard. But he left that he was undergoing a profound change, giving up fiction and going over into the dramatic media. He explained it via another family allusion: his brother Bernard had told him that when he was a little boy, he was naturally left-handed but that he was taught to use his right hand. His fiction, Vonnegut now implied, had been written with his right hand, and now he was going back to explore his long-suppressed left-handedness.

Vonnegut As Playwright

In the spring of 1970, Vonnegut met Lester Goldsmith, former executive at Paramount Pictures and now an independent producer. Goldsmith optioned Vonnegut's *Happy Birthday, Wanda June*, and the writer went home and rewrote the play again (it had been experimentally produced as *Penelope* in 1960, rewritten in 1962, optioned but not produced by Estelle Parsons). In August, Vonnegut said of his script that it was still "a filthy tossed salad of corrasable bond." Michael J. Kane, who had directed Mister Roberts, agreed to direct *Wanda June*; he assembled a cast headed by Kevin McCarthy. During rehearsals in the Theatre de Lys in Greenwich Village, Vonnegut worked in a nearby penthouse borrowed from a friend, writing new drafts of the beginning and the end. The opening night's performance was praised by Clive Barnes, Walter Kerr, Martin Gottfried, and Judith Crist, but two other critics revived an old charge against Vonnegut: John Simon said he was "pandering to youth" and Stanley Kauffman accused him of "dormitory profundity." Vonnegut was miserable, and he was still rewriting in the sixth week of the run. He felt the main trouble with the play was that its author could not make anybody - not even a 1970 Odysseus - thoroughly vile, and such extremes of character can be required in the dramatic format. This particular struggle of Vonnegut's had already figured in his long procrastination with *Slaughterhouse-Five*; he resolved it in the fiction format (as we shall see in some detail later) by making the difficulty of telling the story one of the main **themes** of the story. In November 1970, an off-Broadway actors' strike gave Vonnegut's company a chance to move uptown to the Edison Theatre, where *Wanda June* reopened on December 22 and ran until March 14, 1971.

Vonnegut At Harvard

Meanwhile, in the fall 1970 semester, Vonnegut had also been teaching at Harvard. Announcement that the author of *Slaughterhouse-Five* would teach "English V - Creative Writing" resulted in fifteen applications for each seat in the class. In his lecture-discussion sessions, he wrestled continuously with problems of defining form and artistic purpose. In a public lecture, he read a portion of his abandoned novel-in-progress, *Breakfast of Champions*. This story, according to descriptions that had appeared in earlier interviews, deals with the plight of robots who take over the mid-West but find themselves plagued with questions of free will. The narrator is a real flesh-and-blood person, a Pontiac dealer (we recall that Vonnegut had been a Saab dealer). Vonnegut's Harvard reading began: "I am an experiment by the Creator of the Universe." The narrator went on to describe that moment he first realized that nobody could help doing what he was doing. "Jesus Christ," the narrator was saying, "is a robot who died for my sins." Vonnegut broke off in the middle of a passage and said, "It's never coming out. It bores me stiff." To an editor doing a piece for the *New York Times* Magazine, Vonnegut reiterated his intention of breaking off with fiction altogether. He was now fascinated with the dramatic form known as Commedia dell'Arte and he was forming "Sourdough, Ltd.," with Goldsmith as president, to experiment with movies and video cassettes.

Commedia Dell'Arte

This dramatic **genre** flourished from about 1560 to 1760. Its name means "comedy by profession" because it was developed by serious artists who wanted to distinguish themselves from amateur comedians. They prepared only an outline of a play in advance - usually on the **theme** of true love - and they improvised most of the speech and action. The resultant play -never performed the same way twice - was a racy mixture of satirical dialogue, slapstick farce, clowning, music, and stunts. Vonnegut explained one idea he had in mind for a commedia dell'arte work: the heroine would be a painter of enormous pornographic canvases.

Vonnegut On Tape And Screen

In 1971, *Happy Birthday, Wanda June* opened in New York as a film. Critical consensus was that Vonnegut had not yet found himself in this new medium. In March 1972, he produced *Between Time and Timbuktu: A Space Fantasy on the NET Playhouse*, and it was clear that Vonnegut was adapting fast. And then *Slaughterhouse-Five* was translated to the screen and "this time around, the fates - and the filmmakers - have dealt fairly with a Vonnegut work," as Judith Crist observed in her review. The screenplay had been written by Stephen Geller, George Roy Hill directed, and Michael Sacks played Billy Pilgrim.

Vonnegut's Pilgrimage

Looking back, we can surmise what had happened to Vonnegut. *Slaughterhouse-Five* is his finest statement of his major themes, rendered in an original style that he had been developing and refining for two decades. After publication of this masterpiece, he suffered the natural let-down so often experienced at that point by the creative artist. His urge to express himself in fiction could return. Or it could prove to have run its course. Furthermore, he had always been obliged, for economic reasons, to favor fiction. Yet drama played a major part in his personal development, especially in raising questions about the relationship between art and life, and about our need for both heroes and villains. And now, with the tremendous financial success that followed *Slaughterhouse-Five*, he is for the first time free to experiment with other **genre**, other media. Like an older writer whom he resembles in certain ways - Samuel Beckett -Vonnegut might now, for a while at least, be more concerned with the "painterly" than with the literary.

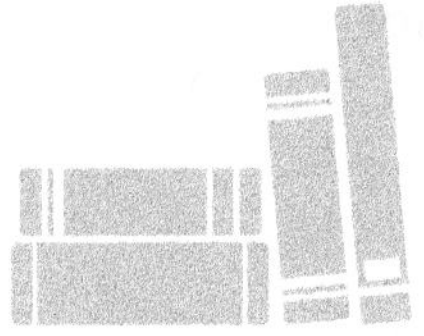

SLAUGHTERHOUSE-FIVE

THEMES AND TECHNIQUES IN SLAUGHTERHOUSE-FIVE

Our textual analysis has shown that, as the story is unraveled and the main character is examined in detail, there emerge several recurrent themes which are stated through a variety of literary techniques. It remains now for us to relate these **themes** into an overall pattern of meaning, and then to study the artistic relationship between the **themes** and the techniques.

TEN MAJOR THEMES

Self-Righteousness Versus Evil

In *Slaughterhouse-Five*, righteousness itself is revealed as a force for evil. In the name of justice, man commits injustice.

Nationalism

Nationality tends to stultify man's basic humanity. It encourages him to ignore the evil in US and the good in THEM: to externalize all evil in THEM. It fosters a false sense of supremacy, especially moral supremacy.

Nature Of War

Its After-Effects. In *Slaughterhouse-Five*, war swiftly reduces a self-righteous avenging nation to the moral level of its enemy. War squashes personality, makes it difficult for a human being to develop his full character potential. The effects of war last long after peace begins: the victim of war, grateful for survival, becomes passive, yielding, a conformist, asking little and asserting himself as little as possible.

War Literature: Art And Artist

The horrors of modern war, we infer from Vonnegut's treatment, are beyond the power of conventional literature to represent fully. And rendering war experience into a traditional format - with its "dramatic" structure and its resultant "comprehension" and containment of the action - has the undesired side-effect of making war attractive, thus helping to perpetuate war. The true horrors of war are best approached by indirection. An account of the artist's difficulties in coming to terms with war can help create a true picture of the effects of war. On certain subjects, we infer from Vonnegut's approach, art must present not results but process. On such subjects, fiction should not strive to present meaningful connections and generalizations. It should present only clusters of images, tendentiously selected by the artist, which the reader may assemble into patterns of experience of his own. The function of art is not to reassure man about purpose or meaning but to enhance his sense of existence.

(The pattern of **themes** presented here is largely our assemblage of our impressions of Vonnegut's images.)

Nature Of Middle-Class Culture

As depicted in *Slaughterhouse-Five,* middle-class life is sterile and hypocritical. It pollutes human relations and esthetic impulse with materialistic considerations. It reduces love, marriage, family life, childhood, womanhood, etc., into mockeries of themselves. Middle-class culture is pictured in *Slaughterhouse-Five* as forcing the individual to deny his own experience and suppress his individuality. It raises machines above man. He is in constant danger of being destroyed by machines supposedly created to serve him.

Mother/Father Worlds; Sexual Differentiation

In *Slaughterhouse-Five* man is pulled between what we have called, for convenience in discussion, the Mother World which stresses human worth, validity of subjective feelings, importance of creativity; and the Father World which stresses social demands, objective logic, rank, judgment, punishment. The best people in the book are those who combine the best of both worlds. But middle-class culture is patriarchal: it subordinates the Mother World and pressures each individual into either an exclusively "masculine" mold or an exclusively "feminine" mold. In middle-class culture, again, the individual is not free to achieve his full (bisexual) human nature.

Accident/Causation; Agent/Victim

In the world-view pervading *Slaughterhouse-Five*, whatever happens is structured by the moment. Man is at best both an agent and a victim, but war tends to make him more a victim.

Breakdown In Communication

In modern life as Vonnegut paints it, communication fails. Man is no longer in touch even with himself. He never fully expresses himself, never fully understands others. The problem is caused partly by society's overemphasis on generalization and abstraction, which insulate man against real experience and make him an easier dupe of self-righteousness. War and modern technology have conspired to make man a thing.

Nature Of Time

Chronological or mechanical time (outer time, "objective time") is represented in the novel as only one measure, one route, of experience. Real time includes psychological time (inner time, "subjective time"), which is not linear but free-flowing and multi-dimensional.

Fragmentation Of Personality

As pictured in *Slaughterhouse-Five*, then, modern man denies his own experience, his nature, his individuality, and lives in a state of explosive self-contradiction, self-suppression, and unfulfillment. He is immobilized, confused, ineffectual, passive, misled. He is no longer capable of "character."

LITERARY TECHNIQUES AND STYLE

Point Of View

Vonnegut tells his story by adopting a double point of view. First he lets us know about the author's own war-time experience so that we will never forget, as we read about his characters' experience, that Vonnegut is spinning a story partly out of his own life materials. Then he stands back, hovering offstage and assumes all the prerogatives of the omniscient narrator. In this role, he is able to be above and beyond the action, telling us things the characters cannot know, giving us broad perspective in time and space, going into the private thoughts of any character as he sees fit. Repeatedly, though, he himself steps back onstage, reminds us that he was once inside the action even though he is now above it.

Narrative Technique

Vonnegut presents his material in a series of apparently unconnected images. He leaves "gaps" between these short bursts of language. In the technical terminology of modern poetry, these "gaps" are "suppressed transitions." The reader is himself supposed to infer transitions, to make equations between the images, to see them as free-associations, to weigh contrasts, see one image as cause, another as effect, and so on. In other words, Vonnegut has deliberately designed his presentation so as to require the reader's active participation. On the title-page he describes this as a novel composed in a "telegraphic, schizophrenic manner." The discrete images, then, are likened to a series of telegrams. But in calling this manner "schizophrenic" Vonnegut is being more ironic than metaphoric. To the conventional mind, which believes that all connections can and should be established objectively, Vonnegut's approach would seem "schizophrenic," that is reflecting an inability to see the connectedness of reality.

Levels Of Narration

As the images multiply, it becomes clearer to us that Vonnegut is presenting images on four levels, concurrently. In addition to (1) the author's problems in telling the story, he is relating (2) the main character's war experiences, (3) the main character's civilian experience, both (3A) pre-war and (3B) post-war, and (4) the main character's fantasy life. Through most of the story, the author uses (2) the main character's wartime adventures as the main level on which to advance his entire story and from which to go forward in time to (3B) Billy's post-war life and back in time to (3A) Billy's pre-war life. But near the end we realize that, of course, the author has unraveled all four levels from the double perspective of the author's and the main-character's backward look, from the vantage point of 1968, at the period 1922–1968. Vonnegut is creatively playing with the nature of time. In retrospect, we can relive a past moment with the added knowledge of the future of that moment. In 1967, Billy can remember what happened in 1945 as though he then had prophetic vision of what was to happen in 1961! One of the points here is that in overlaying the knowledge of one time period on the action of another, we change the objective nature of both periods.

Flexible Perspective

In addition to shifting his action from one level to another, the author maintains flexible distance from each level. He may summarize several years in a sentence, then slow down the action for intensive closeups of one particular moment, giving it more space than he gives the preceding three years.

Linkage

As the story unravels, and we ourselves gain more perspective, we find it easier to perceive at least psychological linkage between the various images: links that explain why or how the main character has free associated from one image to another. Thus, ultimately we see that all the basic materials of Billy's fantasy life are supplied by events of his real life, objects or pictures he has seen, books he has read. And we can see that an unpleasant outer experience, like being imprisoned by Germans inside a boxcar, results in a more serene inner experience, a fantasy of being kidnapped by outer-spacemen in a flying saucer. Any transition in space or vision-like moving from one room to another, or turning on the light-is likely to precipitate a leap across time to a past experience or a leap into fantasy.

Science-Fiction Techniques

For a while it appears that Billy is especially creative in imagining a utopian, extra-terrestrial world which gives him perspective on our own. Later it develops that in these fantasies he puts himself into an outer-space mode of existence created by a writer of science fiction to whose works he has become addicted. The function of the space-fantasy, whether it is being read or being elaborated on after the reading, remains the same. For example, terrestrials make rigid sexual distinctions, which can be inconvenient for Billy, whose weeping is "unmanly" and must be done in private. But extra-terrestrials see not only the need for, but the existence of, as many as five to seven different sexes. Thus if the hard-boiled Marine major belongs in the rigid "masculine" mold, and the passive, formless Valencia belongs in the traditional "feminine" mold, the more complicated Billy can visualize himself in one of the more complex sexes that extra-terrestrials acknowledge. Note that Billy imagines (intuits) that those extra "sexes" are there, even if patriarchal society denies their existence. Science fiction serves Vonnegut as well as it serves the main character. The author is able to establish certain ideas by giving us the plot of certain science-fiction novels that Billy reads. The plot of *The Gutless Wonder*, about the robot-pilot who drops burning gasoline on people but is disliked for his halitosis, gives Vonnegut's reader perspective on the absurd values of "real" life. For both Billy and us, this story implies that any pilot who drops jellied gasoline on women and children must be a robot, and that human beings must have perverted values if their only criticism of this pilot is of his bad breath.

Parable

Vonnegut makes many of his most effective points through parable. A parable is a simple story that illustrates a moral or religious lesson. Usually the parable does its job so well the author need add no comment. The message, or application, of the parable of *The Gutless Wonder* must be inferred and verbalized by the reader himself. Again, Vonnegut uses a technique that requires our participation.

Realism, Surrealism, Satire

Some of the scenes are realistic: they are presented with due regard to historical, objective reality: for example, the combat scenes. Some scenes are surrealistic: they consist of dreams or fantasies presented as though they were really happening: for example, Billy's departure on the space-ship. And some scenes are satiric: that is, somewhat realistic but distorted in a humorous way, in order to hold some human fault up to ridicule or scorn. Consider the scene in which Vonnegut has Valencia say, in all seriousness, that they must pick their silver-pattern carefully because they're going to have to live with it forever. Vonnegut is holding her up to ridicule for her conformity to middle-class emphasis on things and permanence. Another satiric scene is the one in which the coach tearfully says it would be "an honor to be water boy to these kids." This is a succinct **satire** on the maudlin seriousness with which our culture views competitive sports, giving the players a phony heroic quality instead of emphasizing the fun of playing. Campbell's uniform is, of course, a **satire** on chauvinism. In Valencia's speech, in the coach's tears, in Campbell's uniform, Vonnegut has exaggerated something really there in order to make it a target for our contempt.

Black Humor

Black humor is a form of extreme, savage **satire** which makes us laugh so that we will not cry. Its focus is on situations so absurd that we would find them bitterly unbearable unless they were presented humorously. First we laugh, then we look back in dismay or even horror at what we laughed at. The absurd situation of the British prisoners is a typical Black Humor situation. They work so hard to maintain a high morale that they earn the admiration of the Germans, to whom they are proof that war is "reasonable and fun." The Black Humorist in Vonnegut makes us laugh at the British before we shake our heads at the pathos, the **irony** of their plight.

Historical Allusions

Vonnegut uses historical **allusions** as overlays on his main action. This increases the pathos of the human condition; it adds greater depth to the present story. Thus the **allusions** to the Prussians' siege of Dresden in 1760 intensify the horror of the American assault in Dresden in 1945: what was said about the Prussians then becomes applicable to the Americans now. Most bitterly poignant of the historical parallels is that drawn with the Children's Crusade. Not only are Billy and O'Hare likened to the mere children who were led off to death and captivity in 1213, but also authors are satirized for what they do when they write about their war experience: they were immature when they were drafted, but mature when they write about it, so that war literature adds a depth, a profundity, a purpose to the experience that it did not have in actuality.

Biblical Allusions

Vonnegut makes many of his points by alluding, directly or implicitly, to classic, stories in the Bible. He engages here in a form of mythopoeia: the remaking or reinterpreting of myths. The Sodom and Gomorrah story in Genesis is supposed to make us feel that God was right in destroying those "vile people," that the world is "better off without them." Very subtly Vonnegut is able to make us re-think that situation. They were people, after all, and the devastation of whole populations is cruel, no matter what the pretext. Vonnegut makes us realize that our culture has brainwashed us not to see that self-righteous wrath can be tantamount to the cruel evil it obliterates. Of course, again, there is the parallel to a modern city in 1945. Genesis also tells us that Lot's wife was punished for disobeying the order not to look back on the devastated towns. Vonnegut makes us like her for being so human. These reinterpretations of Biblical stories prepare us for the Black Humor **satire** on the New Testament which runs through several chapters. Of course, an extra-terrestrial would find it hard to reconcile Christian behavior with Christian Scripture. The extra-terrestrial's rewriting of the Gospels is one of the most brilliant passages in *Slaughterhouse-Five*. His point that Jesus was a poor human being, a nobody, who was adopted by God must be seen in the light of Vonnegut's twice identifying Billy with Jesus. God's adoption of a suffering nobody is long overdue. But then, in another time-travel story, Vonnegut tells us, in effect, that God is Dead.

Other Literary Allusions

By making several overt literary **allusions** early in the novel, Vonnegut alerts us to expect more veiled **allusions** later on. Roethke, Celine, and Goethe he quotes and comments on directly. Bunyan's *Pilgrim's Progress* he invokes rather obliquely, by naming his main character Billy Pilgrim. But some of the most powerful **allusions** are implicit. For the reader who senses them, they add resonances to the story. Thus the tens of thousands of American prisoners, stretched in meandering columns all the way to the horizon, "moaning and sighing," invoke our recollections of Dante's *Inferno*. And the war adventures of Roland Weary parallel and **parody** *The Song of Roland*. For the reader who sees the parallel, Vonnegut has made a telling contrast between the propagandistic glamorizing of medieval war-poems and the sordid absurdity of real war as Vonnegut sees it. The student will find it profitable also to explore the parallels with the rain scene in Hemingway's *Farewell to Arms* and with both **themes** and treatment in Hesse's *Journey to the East*.

Description And Diction

Although he has been criticized for failing to give us a full realistic treatment (see "Critics Respond to *Slaughterhouse-Five*"), the fact is that whenever it serves his purpose, Vonnegut gives up unforgettable descriptions. These are more suggestive than documentary. Nevertheless, we have indelible impressions of the prisoner-of-war camp at night, the war-film run backward, the men hiding in the forest and being shelled by the Germans. In the case of the night-scene in camp, Vonnegut achieves his effect partly by emphasizing the weirdly minimal lighting but mainly by making us aware of the design of the camp: it consists in effect of a system of conduits for directing this slow flow of sad humanity. Vonnegut achieves a brilliant contrast with the British prisoners by using vivid language that races and sparkles: rodomontades, azure curtains, darling elves. And with the film-in-reverse and the plight of the men under shellfire, Vonnegut achieves his effects by using an unwordly vocabulary: he calls anti-aircraft guns long steel tubes and bullets lumps of lead in copper jackets, and the death-filled air is the incredible artificial weather that Earthlings sometimes create for other Earthlings when they don't want those other Earthlings to inhabit Earth any more. Such **diction** forces us to look close, and fresh, at very familiar things, as though we were reading a report for non-Earthlings.

Contrasts And Equations

Trying to explain the effectiveness of apparently simple descriptions, we realize that it is attributable in part to Vonnegut's deft use of contrast. Note how the contrast between the ugly American Roland Weary and the beautiful German androgyne adds to the description of both! Note how Dresden is partly described by telling us what has happened to other cities! And notice how the American prisoners in Dresden are poised against the Austrian skiers in Vermont to balance off war against peace and soldiers' fate vs. civilians' freedom. These artistic balances are sometimes rendered in the form of dream equations, as when, for example, Billy's fantasy of his being killed by Lazzaro, in vengeance for Weary's death, results in an extrapolation to the international level: his country is Balkanized for having posed threats to world peace.

Metaphor And Symbolism

That so much can be packed into only 186 pages is due largely to Vonnegut's mastery of figures of speech. Events and situations are described in terms of what they are not. The shock to the reader - of assimilating a similarity between dissimilars - makes the description both memorable and emotional. We remember the dying Colonel's coughing because it is likened to something we know but did not expect to hear: his lungs rattled like greasy paper bags. We get the sight and the feel of the sleeping prisoners because they nestled like spoons. We understand how Tralfamadorians view time because they can see it spread out like the Rocky Mountains. The most veiled artistry, though, is in symbolism, the investing of some material thing with the values of something immaterial. The coats and shoes that prisoners must accept, willy-nilly, symbolize the way war transforms individual people into interchangeable identities. The wrong-number call, late at night, becomes the dead-end of communication. The Church of our Lady, standing amidst the ruins, and the syrup for pregnant women, both represent the values of the Mother World amidst the havoc wrought by the Father World. Almost every scene, situation, and object in *Slaughterhouse-Five* takes on an additional value. When the Austrian skis up to the plane with its

28 dead bodies he hears Billy saying "Schlachthof." Indeed, the plane is a slaughterhouse.

Style And Syntax

His **diction**, his symbolism and figures of speech, his suggestiveness, his covert contrasts and allusions, all these stylistic ingredients do not become vintage Vonnegut until they are rendered in his peculiar **syntax**. Compare the typical modern writer with Vonnegut. The typical writer varies greatly both the length and the structure of his sentences. He will make some sentences short, some medium-length, some long. Some he will make simple, with just one clause; others compound, with two equal clauses; and many complex, with a main clause and one or more subordinate clauses. Sometimes he will begin a sentence with the subject, more often though with a modifier of some kind or even with a dependent clause.

Vonnegut is different right down the line. He makes most of his sentences short, some medium-length, very few of them long. He makes an unusually large number of them simple, an unusually small number of them complex. He opens, more often than not, with the subject. This is the perfect equivalent, on the level of **syntax** (arrangement of sentence elements), of his larger structure, or overall arrangement of scenes and sequences. Just as he prefers to use short scenes, parables, anecdotes and notions not overtly connected, leaving the reader to make transitions and relations, so he chooses to use simple sentences with as few conjunctions as possible, leaving the reader to make both connections and emphases.

The Vonnegut style looks easy. Anybody who tries it for the first time will discover that it's easy to express simple ideas this way but very difficult to express complex ones! And Vonnegut chooses to express complex ideas in simple **syntax**. As a consequence, he must be selective and laconic, with tongue in cheek, ingenious in the juxtaposition of statements, making the most of figures of speech, parables and parallels, striving always for concentration, vividness, resonance. The technique of course is well known to poets. It's no surprise to learn that Vonnegut was reading Edgar Lee Master's *Spoon-River Anthology* when he was twelve.

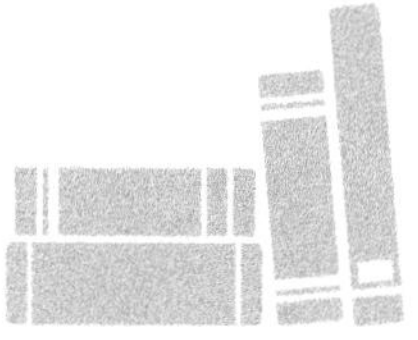

SLAUGHTERHOUSE-FIVE

TEXTUAL ANALYSIS

CHAPTER 1

MANNER

We experience a double-surprise in reading chapter 1. Both the manner and the matter are unusual. The author expresses himself in a series of comments, recollections, images, allusions. But he leaves "gaps" between these short bursts of language. He himself remains silent about the most significant connections between these images. He leaves it to us to assemble these impulses into patterns of ideas. We realize now that Vonnegut has deliberately designed his work so as to require our participation. We recall that on the title page he has described this as a novel composed in a "telegraphic, schizophrenic manner."

MATTER

The subject matter is also strange. The novel will be about the author's war experiences. But he and his buddy cannot talk about them directly. We soon realize that the author's difficulty in writing his novel will constitute one of the main themes. What we are reading in this chapter could sound like an introduction or preface, and some critics makes the mistake of calling it that. But it is not a separate introduction, it is a chapter, it is clearly headed "1," it is organically related to 2 and 5 and 10. Vonnegut simply will not separate his story from the problems of the story-teller.

Several other **themes** are also suggested in this chapter, some of which do not seem at the moment to be relevant. Regular readers of Vonnegut will recognize some of them as his perennial preoccupations. Let's identify all these **themes** and motifs - that is, translate the images into ideas - before we examine some of them in detail.

THEMES AND MOTIFS

The main themes, apparently, are the nature of war and its aftermath and the nature of art and the artist's relation to his work. The author also seems preoccupied with: the relationship between man and his machines; man's tension in his double role as both agent and victim; the relationship between accident and causation; the nature of time; the nature of human communications; the relationship between self-righteousness and evil; the differences between "Father-World" and "Mother-World."

NATURE OF WAR

Almost everything in this chapter - characterization, historical allusions, reminiscences of war buddies, and the author's tone -

contributes to our overall impression that the author regards war as the ultimate idiocy and the ultimate evil. Note that much of the effect here is accomplished in terms of embarrassment. O'Hare is embarrassed that Vonnegut is trying to exploit their war experiences for his "trade" as a writer; both men are embarrassed at the simple, unanswerable truth of Mary's insight into the machismo of men's war reminiscences. The reader is embarrassed, for all mankind, to learn that Pope Innocent III could actually have said, in his enthusiasm over the Children's Crusade, "These children are awake while we are asleep!" The deepest hurt in such revelations is that proper embarrassment comes only with hindsight. Man is a prisoner of time who learns relevant facts, gains proper perspective, too late. This makes man the likely dupe of unacknowledged schemes, of hasty generalizations and oversimplifications, and makes Vonnegut doubtful about the wisdom of any all-out crusade or any generalization. Not the least of the idiocies is the American government's insistence, years after the war, that the massacre of 135,000 civilians in an open city was still "top secret." Silence at the top covers up a different kind of embarrassment.

NATURE OF ART: RESULT OR PROCESS?

Vonnegut's refusal to separate the difficulty of telling his story from the story proper reflects one of the most significant developments in avant-garde art. The artist can no longer make an artificial distinction between the result of his artistry and its process. If he is to reveal anything like the truth, it must include means as well as ends. This accounts in part for the prevalence of the confessional mode in today's literature: we cannot comprehend the Creation unless we see it in dynamic relation to its Creator. Some readers will see here a parallel between Vonnegut's *Slaughterhouse-Five* and Hermann Hesse's *Journey to the East* in which the difficulty of writing about the quest for an ideal becomes as important a **theme** as the quest itself. But in Hesse's novel the "difficulty" theme emerges late; in Vonnegut's novel the problem in facing the material is acknowledged immediately as part of the material. And since process is to be emphasized, we appreciate the wisdom of involving the reader in the struggle for conclusions.

EFFECT OF WAR LITERATURE

Apparently Vonnegut had been unconscious of one of the deepest reasons for his procrastination in writing his war novel. He was made conscious of it as a result of dialogue (process). Ironically, this insight came from dialogue not with the war-buddy he went to interview, but with the war-buddy's wife. Mary knows that when a veteran sits down at last to write his war novel he will impose upon the immaturity of his days as a soldier all the maturity of the older writer, so that the war experience will be imbued with a greater sense of purpose, dignity, and nobility than it really had. Again, Vonnegut - like Hesse and Samuel Beckett - is made wary of the unpredictable effects of the artist's human tendency to rationalize and synthesize. Again we see the wisdom of letting the reader make his own formulations. In the past, many writers - Hemingway, Mailer, to name a few - wrote about their wartime experiences in an honest effort to make sense of them. But more recently, authors have had to face the ironic possibility that even an anti-war novel (like Erich Remarque's *All Quiet on the Western Front*) can - if it describes war realistically - create a curiosity about war, contribute to the mystique of war, so that one effect of any war literature can be to help perpetuate war. We should recall here how the heroine of Doris Lessing's *The Golden Notebook* is appalled when her first novel has actually instilled in her readers a nostalgia for war! This miscarriage of artistic intention is enough to make Anna Wulf stop writing until she has better understanding of the effect and function of literature.

EFFECT OF "PLOT" STRUCTURE

Note that Vonnegut further dramatizes these difficulties in terms of his early efforts to shape his war experiences into a traditional plot: with rising action, **climax**, **denouement** and, it is implied, catharsis. O'Hare is embarrassed, of course. Such a "rational" arrangement would suggest some cause and effect, some human motivation, some progress and resolution. It would impose a meaning on what both men regard as having been absurd, chaotic, obscene events. There is nothing intelligent to say about a massacre. Traditional story form, in handling such atrocities, in effect dominates them, contains them, reduces them to something comprehensible and finite. The war-buddies, we sense from their attitude, know that their knowledge of Dresden cannot be contained. It is infinite and incomprehensible.

Such a plot structure as Vonnegut was contemplating would also have required a clear-cut conflict between the forces of "good" and "evil." Vonnegut himself would have to "take sides" in order to identify these forces, incarnate them in a hero and a villain maybe. But Vonnegut slyly uses the story of Sodom and Gomorrah to illustrate what the difficulty would be for him. The Bible assumes that God was right in utterly destroying the two cities, in reducing the inhabitants as well as the buildings to ash. "Those were vile people, as is well known," Vonnegut concludes. "The world was better off without them." Nevertheless, the way he has told the story makes us realize that they were still people, after all, and that the wrath of self-righteousness can itself be tantamount to evil. Vonnegut's sympathies for all people make it impossible for him to structure a story according to a conflict between the allegedly "good" ones and the allegedly "bad" ones. Again, God turned Lot's wife into a pillar of salt because she succumbed to the human temptation to look back "where all those people ... had been" and again, Vonnegut's sympathies are not with the powerful avenger of "wrongs" but with the powerless victim of vengeance.

Of all the unarticulated meanings in Vonnegut's retelling of the Sodom and Gomorrah story, the most horrible is that the people who rained fire and brimstone upon Dresden in 1945 were arrogating to themselves the privileges of a vengeful God. And not even God had that right, Vonnegut seems to say. Anyhow, "Sodom and Gomorrah" is a typical plotted story: the forces of "good" in their crusade against the "vile": **climax**, triumph, catharsis, and these are the reasons Vonnegut can't write such a story.

MAN AS AGENT/VICTIM

Also present in this seemingly casual first chapter is Vonnegut's concern for man in his double role as someone who thinks like a "free agent" but actually is often manipulated. Not only the children in the Children's Crusade thought they were going to Palestine, the Pope thought they were too, and he even had that beautiful insight into the children's superior insight! And all 30,000 of them were pawns of two monks turned slave-herders! Note that Vonnegut's view of man's ambiguous role determines the very quality of his **diction**. "Thousands of us," he recalls, were "about to stop being prisoners of war." To stop being is a very neutral phase, implying neither desire nor compulsion, although both were there.

ACCIDENT/CAUSATION

Closely related to the **theme** of man as agent/victim is Vonnegut's concern over man's belief that a distinction can be made between accident and purpose. The German cabdriver's quaint command of English produces, ironically, the clause: "If the accident will." As readers of *Cat's Cradle* already know, everything that happens had to happen; everybody does what he has to do. A true Bokononist never says: "As it happened..." but instead "As it was supposed to happen... ."

NATURE OF COMMUNICATION

Vonnegut gives us several signals about man's problems with communication: note his fascination with the underground network of pneumatic tubes and his continual efforts to locate old acquaintances through the "information" operator. More significant perhaps are the "white lies" (foma) that O'Hare tells and the author's observation that what Mary said aloud was a mere "fragment of a ... larger conversation." And central to this **theme** is Vonnegut's recollection that he thought it would be "easy to write about the destruction of Dresden," because all he would have to do would be to report what he had seen! Vonnegut's overall attitude toward the possibility of communication reminds us of the doctrine of an ancient philosopher, Gorgias of Lentini (483-375 B.C.): "Nothing has any real existence; even if it did exist, it could not be known; even if anything could be known, it could not be communicated." The last part implies that it is impossible for any idea to take the same shape in different minds.

NATURE OF TIME

Part of the communication problem is that men live by different modes of time. Notice how Vonnegut makes us progressively more aware of this: at the World's Fair, he is prompted to consider past and future and especially how wide and deep the present is. This is the way we describe a river: now we know why the girls were so intent on staring at the Hudson: it symbolizes chronological time, linear time that flows in one direction. But later, in the motel, the author has strange experiences with his watch: the second-hand would twitch and a year would pass. Vonnegut is cuing us for a journey into psychological time. Henri Bergson formulated the distinction nicely for us, and writers like Ambrose Bierce ("Incident at Owl Creek Bridge") and Virginia Woolf (*Orlando*) have exploited it ever since. Mechanical or chronological time assigns equal value to each minute or each unit; but human experience can be wider and deeper one minute, narrow and shallow the next; we can pack a decade into a summer or grow only an hour in a lean year: this kind of time, psychological time, Bergson considered to be time closer to reality. It can, of course, flow back and forth: it uses the present as a stage for both recollection and anticipation and fantasy, and it blends them all. And this flow, Bergson pointed out, is a flow of discrete images. Vonnegut ends the chapter with the cue that Billy Pilgrim has come "unstuck in time." In terms of the connections we have already made, this means he will not be a prisoner of chronological time, with the embarrassments of hindsight. He will have perspective which may tell us a lot about the human condition.

AUTHOR'S FLEXIBLE PERSPECTIVE

Vonnegut, we realize, has already structured even chapter 1 that way. He has free-associated back and forth across time and has taken full advantage of flexible perspective. Much of his experience as a reporter is concentrated into a swift sentence or two. Then he circles back and slows down and zooms in on one story that he covered: the elevator accident. Again, he outlines years of his war experience in a paragraph, then slows down and zooms in for a close-up of one **episode**: the exchange of prisoners in the beetfield.

HISTORICAL ALLUSIONS

Vonnegut has also prepared us for simultaneity of past-present-future by using historical **allusions** in depth. Mary's comments about how the veterans forget they were only children during the war prompts Vonnegut to include the analogy of the Children's Crusade in both his title and his action. (Reader's familiar with Hesse will again see parallels here to *Journey to the East* in which the narrator describes his pilgrimage as a "Children's Crusade," a pilgrimage in which the pilgrims "creatively brought the past, the future and the fictitious into the present moment." The historical Children's Crusade took place about the year 1213 A.D. It was one in a series of crusades, the others all composed of "grown-ups," which began just before 1100 A.D. and lasted until nearly 1300 A.D. The purpose was to wrest control of the Holy City of Jerusalem from the Moslems. The Christian Crusaders took the City, then the Moslems re-took it. Then the Christians re-took it, ad nauseam. One of the multiple ironies in Vonnegut's use of the Children's Crusade is that to this day most people are not aware of the truth about it: namely, that it was engineered to lure thousands of children (most of them under twelve!) en masse into slavery. The parallel with Dresden resonates: for years after Dresden, the Allied governments tried to suppress the facts about the atrocity, and until *Slaughterhouse-Five* appeared most Americans had only the vaguest knowledge of the fire raid. Vonnegut's **allusion** to the siege of Dresden in 1760 also provides historical resonance. Devastation of the city - especially its arts and architecture - proved pointless because Friedrich of Prussia had finally to rush off to fight another battle elsewhere.

LITERARY ALLUSIONS

The way literature figures in Vonnegut's process also helps establish the simultaneity of all experience. Most of his literary **allusions** are explicit: Vonnegut intends, of course, to evoke our memories of the full story of Sodom and Gomorrah, of Lot and his wife, in Genesis: 18:16–19:29. The poem *Words for the Wind* by Theodore Roethke is also important for its multiple ironies. Roethke describes, in the first line, the state of sleep as the real state of consciousness, and the state of being awake as the real unconsciousness. In sleep, of course, we are in touch with the "forgotten language" of symbols and in dreams we enjoy simultaneity of all time periods. Thus Vonnegut further prepares us for Billy Pilgrim's state of being "unstuck," while he also reminds us of the Pope's innocent **irony** in describing the child-pilgrims as "awake while we sleep." Roethke's second line seems to imply that fate comes in the most natural disguise, as something one would not normally be afraid of, so one would not recognize it as fate! The third line, expressing Roethke's idea that he learns from what he has to do, again emphasizes man's need to be in touch with his own nature. The reference to Erika Ostrovsky's *Celine and his Vision* serves several purposes. Louis-Ferdnand Celine was a French soldier in World War I who suffered a crack on the head that changed his entire life: we shall have occasion to think of Celine's "vision" later in connection with Billy Pilgrim's "visions." Furthermore, time obsessed Celine, and of course Vonnegut is inviting us to observe that time obsesses Vonnegut. Celine's wanting to stop the bustling of a street crowd (in Death on the Installment Plan) expresses man's poignant, paradoxical desire to arrest time and change, a desire which can only result in stasis or death. Vonnegut's reference to Celine's belief that no art is possible without a dance with death is another effort of our author to come to grips, somehow, with his subject, to perform his duty as a writer. We have now at last come to understand the full significance of the title and two sub-titles: *Slaughterhouse-Five*: or *The Children's Crusade; a Duty-Dance with Death*.

The Latin quotation Vonnegut uses as he tries to recall the exact year of the World's Fair is the opening line of a famous poem by Horace:

> Eheu, fugaces labuntur anni ... Alas, the fleeing years glide by ...
>
> (Odes, II, 14)

And the quotation from Goethe's comments on the devastation in Dresden in 1760 fits beautifully into Vonnegut's mosaic of images. The passage - pointedly left in the original German - recounts Goethe's visit to the cupola of the Church of our Lady which had withstood the bombardment. There the sexton boasted to Goethe about the magnificent work of the architect. Then, pointing to the "sad ruins" on all sides, the sexton said laconically: "That is the work of the enemy!" In these overlays of past-present-future, we are to see the architectural wonders of 1945, and the "work" of the Americans in destroying them. This contrast between the creative spirit and the destructive urge has another, symbolic, meaning which we shall examine later.

There are also several implicit literary allusions. We have mentioned the parallels with Hesse (Vonnegut published an article on Hesse in Horizon magazine in 1970). There are others for the knowing reader. Vonnegut's injunction to his sons, that the "news of massacres of enemies is not to fill them with satisfaction or glee," is a paraphrase of a passage in Job's famous "Oath of Clearance":

> If I have rejoiced at the ruin of him that hated me, Or exulted when evil overtook him ...
>
> (Job: 31:29)

a passage often referred to as the "high point of ethics in the ancient world." Vonnegut's **allusion** reminds us how we reached the low point of ethics in the modern world by exulting in a victory that included the "ruin" of an open city of our enemies. Finally, Vonnegut makes a veiled **allusion** to a famous passage in Ernest Hemingway's *Farewell to Arms*. Twice Vonnegut tells us that the ceremony of exchanging prisoners was conducted in the rain. We cannot help referring back to that ceremony Hemingway describes, when soldiers standing in formation in the rain were embarrassed to hear citations read that contained obscene words like "honor," "glory," "valor," "sacrifice not made in vain," and so on. Vonnegut and his hero are in a direct line of dropouts that began with Lieutenant Henry on that day in the rain in *Farewell to Arms*.

CHARACTERIZATION

Vonnegut has already created quite a variety of characters by using telling details and significant contrasts. Paul Lazzaro, for example, is swiftly sketched as the kind of human rodent that profits from war and death. Bernard O'Hare is sketched largely through contrast. While Lazzaro's loot from the war is a quart of gems stolen from dead people in Dresden, and Vonnegut (always the ironist) has kept a "ceremonial Luftwaffe saber" (what could be more idiotic in the Air Force than a saber?), O'Hare has taken no souvenir or "trophies" at all. While Vonnegut is ecstatic over a great idea for the "**climax**" of his novel, O'Hare says only "Um." A major contrast runs through the entire cast of characters: Mary and Lot's wife represent the Great Mother who thinks always in terms of human values. Jehovah and the sneering ex-lieutenant-colonel represent the Father World: they are interested primarily in the "social" values of justice, vengeance, logic, and hierarchical rank. Both O'Hare and Vonnegut represent that modern man who has crossed the line and adopted some of the humane values and sensitivity of the Mother World. Vonnegut has also already crossed the line in other ways: he casually tells us that from nicotine and alcohol he sometimes has a "breath like mustard gas and roses" and sometimes he listens to talk-shows on the radio. Later we shall realize one function of these details: to prepare us to see Billy Pilgrim as partly his Creator.

SYMBOLISM

Rivers, as we have noted, symbolize for Vonnegut the flow of time. The Frauenkirche (Church of our Lady) standing intact above the devastation of Dresden also has symbolic value: the Church of our Lady represents the creative urge of the Mother World, the ruins bespeak the destructive power of (Jehovah's) Father World. In short, every last detail in this seemingly "random" collection of images and **allusions** contributes to a consistent pattern of ideas.

SLAUGHTERHOUSE-FIVE

TEXTUAL ANALYSIS

CHAPTER 2

Reading the second chapter, we realize how Vonnegut's seemingly casual first chapter has thoroughly and economically prepared us for many of the **themes** and techniques to follow.

TAG-NAMES

The two main characters in this chapter are "tagged" with names intended to bring literary and historical parallels to the reader's mind. The name Billy Pilgrim connotes John Bunyan's allegorical novel *Pilgrim's Progress* (1678, 1684). It also reminds us of those pre-adolescents who became "pilgrims" in the ghastly Children's Crusade. The name Roland Weary connotes the great hero of early French literature, the title character in the *Song of Roland* (twelfth century, author unknown). The name of Billy Pilgrim's hometown is also a tag-name: Ilium is the classical name for ancient Troy (Homer's *Iliad* is about the Trojan War). **Irony**: the citadel of Troy was conquered by Achaeans who then went back to Greece where soon their great citadels were overrun by invaders. Troy symbolizes the historical fact that those who live by the sword die by the sword in an endless game of "King of the Hill."

PILGRIM'S PROGRESS

Bunyan's novel is an allegory, which is to say, the narrative offers a sustained symbolic parallel. The hero is named Christian and his journey in search of the Celestial City symbolizes the spiritual life of man. Every character and location is "tagged" with an image-making name: Christian meets Giant Despair and Mr. By-Ends; he sees the Slough of Despond, the River of Death; and of course, he triumphs in the Celestial City. Every incident has its double significance; for example, just as Christian comes up to the Cross, his burdens slip from his back, close to the mouth of the tomb, where they fall in, and he sees them no more. This novel, which has been translated into more than 100 languages, is remarkable for its vivid pictures of English life, its down-to-earth characters, and the author's genial regard for humanity.

BILLY PILGRIM'S PROGRESS

In naming Billy Pilgrim so as to remind us of *Pilgrim's Progress*, Vonnegut establishes a literary precedent for "tag" names and of course intends an ironic contrast between Christian's life of purpose, discovery, and meaning and Billy's life of victimization and escape.

SONG OF ROLAND

This great narrative poem (Chanson de Roland) concerns the last stand of Roland, nephew of Charlemagne and one of that emperor's leading generals. Ganelon, another French leader, conspires with the "pagan" enemy to bring about Roland's downfall. Roland is placed in command of the rear-guard forces covering the return of Charlemagne's army from Spain to France. The Saracens or Mohammedans, to whom Ganelon has given the details of Roland's line of march, surprise and overwhelm Roland's outnumbered forces. Oliver, Roland's wise and faithful friend, begs Roland to blow the horn that will signal trouble and bring the main body of Charlemagne's army back to their rescue. But out of pride - and overconfidence, for Roland relishes the chance to defeat the entire Mohammedan army - Roland refuses to blow the horn. The two friends are almost the last Frenchmen left standing when now Roland wants to sound the horn to let Charlemagne know what has happened. And now Oliver dissents on the ground of honor! Roland has refused to summon Charlemagne to the rescue, and now it would be shameful to summon him to see a stupid disaster! In their dying hour, the friends become embittered with each other, almost estranged. Weary as he is, Roland blows the horn and bursts his temples. The angels descend to take his soul into heaven.

Vonnegut's alluding to this poem by calling one of Billy Pilgrim's fellow soldiers Roland Weary further develops some of Vonnegut's **themes** and helps characterize Private Weary. First of all, the *Song of Roland* has its horrific overtones for the reader who has been alerted by Vonnegut to re-read the Sodom and Gomorrah story from a humanitarian point of view. The Christian cause is represented, without question, as absolutely just. The Saracen cause is, absolutely without question, absolutely unjust. No angels descend to take to Heaven any of the thousands of Saracens that Roland has slain. God is on the side of the hero; God is against the villain. This story, like the Sodom and Gomorrah story, exemplifies the ethical fallacies in the traditional plot as Vonnegut sees them.

SONG OF ROLAND WEARY

Notice how Vonnegut develops his parallel between Private Weary and Charlemagne's Roland: (1) Private Weary had a whistle he wasn't going to show to anybody until he got promoted. This corresponds, in an ironic way, to Roland's horn that he wasn't going to blow until his victory or his martyrdom was accomplished. (2) Private Weary imagines that he and the two scouts are as inseparable as The Three Musketeers. This parodies the heroic inseparability of the friends Oliver and Roland. (3) The Germans have no trouble following Privates Weary, Pilgrim, et alia because they leave tracks in the snow. The Saracens had no trouble following Roland whose route they knew beforehand. (4) Finally, when Private Weary berates Billy Pilgrim, blaming him for their loss of their two fellow soldiers, Weary talks of the "great services [The Three Musketeers] rendered to Christianity." When he looks up, Weary sees he is about to be taken by the Germans. When the real Roland completed his services to Christianity, he was "taken" by the angels. Roland Weary's combat career is a **parody** of Chanson de Roland. (The parallel will reach its **denouement** in chapter 3 when Billy Pilgrim the pacifist-rather than Roland Weary the sadist - will look at a young German soldier and see "a blond angel".)

AUTOBIOGRAPHICAL ELEMENTS: RECURRENCE

In addition to his historical and literary sources, Vonnegut uses in chapter 2 some autobiographical details and some elements from his own earlier writing. Billy Pilgrim's life parallels Kurt Vonnegut's in many ways: they were both born in 1922, both stand well over six feet; they both went from college into the Army, both were captured in the Battle of the Bulge, discharged in 1945, and both returned to college and were married soon after. Other details of the author's life are used in portrayal of other characters: Kurt Vonnegut Sr., for example, was a "gun nut," and this side of the author's father appears in Roland Weary's father; Vonnegut and O'Hare were scouts who wandered around behind the German lines, and two of Billy's companions are scouts. Vonnegut's scientific education is reflected in his ease in using technical **imagery**: e.g., his description of Billy Pilgrim's spinal cord, and his measuring of Billy's life span on the spectrum, with birth at the red end and death at the violet end. Billy's home town of Ilium has been the scene of action of Vonnegut's first novel (*Player Piano*), and it corresponds to the town of Schenectady where Vonnegut once worked for General Electric. The Planet Tralfamadore, where Billy finds refuge from the agonies of chronological time on Earth, is known to regular readers of Vonnegut as the home of the intergalactic messenger Salo in The Sirens of Titan.

NARRATIVE TECHNIQUE

The narration follows the structure we were conditioned for in both the manner and the matter of chapter 1. The story is told partly in chronological time and largely in psychological time. It consists of apparently discrete images, quotations, thumbnail sketches, etc., which take us back and forth across time, from history to fantasy, fact to fiction. The camera now "pans" overbroad vistas of time and space, then "zooms in" for a fully dramatized scene. The multi-level nature of any given moment of action - levels which cannot be accurately represented in a linear chronicle - is indicated once when Vonnegut halts the action to detail the "orchestration of the moment." What follows is an account of the congeries of assumptions, experiences, hypotheses and problems that make up Barbara's attitude toward her father.

STYLE AND IMAGERY

Vonnegut's simple sentences, deceptively casual in structure, contain a wealth of figurative language. Typical of his **similes** (figures of speech that make an overt comparison by means of an "equal sign" like like or as) is the conclusion of his description of Billy Pilgrim: He looked like a filthy flamingo. Typical of Vonnegut's **metaphors** (figures in which comparison is made implicitly, without an equal sign) is his description of the bullet: lethal bee that buzzed past his ear. Typical of Vonnegut's use of the **metaphysical** conceit (a **simile** that involves a grotesque, hence more memorable, comparison) is his description of the sound the anti-tank gun made: a ripping sound like the opening of the zipper on the fly of God Almighty. Vonnegut also employs the oxymoron (a figure of speech that surprises us into accepting the union of apparently paradoxical terms, like make haste slowly: the apparently moronic advice proves to be quite sharp!). He describes the scouts as living from moment to moment in useful terror.

SELF-RIGHTEOUSNESS vs. EVIL

Vonnegut ramifies his important **theme** of the evil nature of self-righteousness in several ways. It is manifest in **allusions** to the self-righteousness of *The Song of Roland* and in the speech of Private Roland Weary. It is manifest most horribly in Billy's reading, in *The Execution of Private Slovik*, an account of the death before an American firing-squad of a soldier whose alleged cowardice was considered a challenge to the authority of the government. The cool decision of a military judge-that the "death penalty ... should be imposed ... to maintain that discipline upon which alone an army can succeed" - is a variation on Jehovah's premeditated destruction of Sodom and Gomorrah, and another

foreshadowing of the cool military decision to destroy 135,000 people in the undefended city of Dresden.

CHARACTERIZATION

Vonnegut uses various techniques to delineate his minor characters. He swiftly but unforgettably "types" Billy's mother: Like so many Americans, she was trying to construct a life that made sense from things she found in gift shops. Vonnegut portrays Roland Weary as a person trapped in a role in a neurotic game, like those Eric Berne describes in *Games People Play*. The script is written for Roland, and he re-enacts it endlessly: he is so fearful of being "ditched" that he repeatedly seeks out a person even more unpopular than himself, feigns friendship, and then finds an excuse to violently "ditch the victim of his game. Far from being an unfair or inartistic method of characterization, this use of "pattern" takes on great validity in the light of the researches of Eric Berne, R. D. Laing, and other psychiatrists. With his major character, Billy Pilgrim, Vonnegut uses every artistic technique of characterization compatible with his philosophy: he gives Billy the fullest biographical background of any character and he has Billy reveal his personality both through regular confrontations with others and through his fantasy life. Billy's early biography is a typical middle-class success story: unquestioning service to God and country, preparation for a respectable profession, marriage, children. Vonnegut makes good use of symbolism in choosing Billy's profession: he is an optometrist who helps people improve their vision, first (when he is still respectable), their physical and vision, later (when he is no longer respectable), their philosowphical and spiritual vision. In his confrontation with his father, who believed in teaching children to swim by throwing them in the water, Billy was numb (it was like an execution: the word reminds us of Private Slovik's confrontation with authority). Yielding obediently, Billy almost drowns. In his relationship with the army, Billy is still yielding and obedient, a passive victim of war. In his relationship with the scouts, Billy is unselfish: eager not to hold them back, not to inconvenience them with his troubles. In his confrontation with the sadistic Roland Weary, Billy reveals himself as pacifistic. Billy's confrontations with his daughter reveal the strongest contrast of all. Barbara is fact-bound, conventional, more worried about "what people think" than about what is really wrong with her father. Billy, on the other hand, is equally defending his right to his own beliefs and illusions, calmly and tolerantly trying to bring his "fourth-dimension" vision to others. In the soldiers' fantasy life in combat, we again have revelation through contrast: Roland Weary's fantasies are of triumph at the expense of others, who are proved to be inferior and contemptible. Billy's fantasies are of triumphs over his own weaknesses: he conquers his physical awkwardness and becomes a graceful "skater," he overcomes his poor speaking voice by taking a course in public speaking!

BILLY AND TRALFAMADORE

But what does the main fantasy of Billy's life-his recurrent adventure on Tralfamadore-signify? At this point in the story, we really are in a better position to enjoy the suspense than to attempt answers to that question. For future use, though, we should note that Vonnegut has provided plenty of plausible motivation for Billy's "escapism." From both his family ("sink or swim") and his government (Private Slovik was executed as a warning to you!), Billy has learned that individual desires must be suppressed. Conformity has not brought happiness, and yearnings must still find fulfillment. In Billy's Tralfamadore he finds what 20th Century "progress" has failed to provide:

serenity. Given the **foreshadowing** in chapter 1, and Billy's experiences in chapter 2, we can see Tralfamadore as an answer to Dresden. If the reader finds it an unsatisfactory answer, that may be one of the conclusions the author intended: can't human imagination do something better with technology than Dresden at one extreme and escapist fantasy at the other?

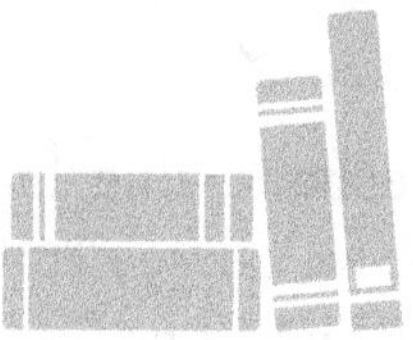

SLAUGHTERHOUSE-FIVE

TEXTUAL ANALYSIS

CHAPTER 3

In his third chapter, Vonnegut especially develops three of his themes: self-righteousness as itself an evil; the differences between the Father World and Mother World; and Man versus Machines. He further develops the social basis for Billy's "schizophrenia" and establishes specific links between Billy's fantasy life and his "real" life.

POINT OF VIEW

Vonnegut maintains his double point of view. On the one hand, he is the author omniscient, sufficiently beyond the immediate action so that he can tell us things Billy cannot know: for example, that the war will be over in six months or that the German patrol's dog's name is "Princess." On the other hand, Vonnegut reminds us "I was there": he is also in the action, at Billy's side. One of the many effects of this double point of view is to remind us that the artist has a good degree of Tralfamadorian perspective.

NARRATIVE TECHNIQUES

Now that it serves his purpose, Vonnegut provides parallels, or establishes psychological links, between the images of Billy's fantasy life and the other images of the author's narrative. We notice that when Billy is closed up in a box-car as a prisoner of war being transported into enemy territory is the time when he is kidnapped by Tralfamadorians and taken aboard a flying saucer into outer space. This linkage helps Vonnegut make his point that Billy's schizophrenia (crudely, a mental state of being divorced from the nature of outer reality) is a reaction to social conditions too horrible to contemplate directly.

SELF-RIGHTEOUSNESS AND EVIL

This chapter bristles with more examples of how the forces of righteousness commit evil in the course of their "punishment" of evil. The Marine major sees the United States as fighting until the Communists "realize" they cannot "force their way of life on weak countries"; if necessary, the U.S. should bomb North Vietnam back into the Stone Age if it refuses to "see reason." In his self-righteousness, the major does not understand that he is himself advocating forcing a way of life on others and that such tactics put his own country back into the Stone Age. Far from enhancing the "cause" of reason, such tactics only renew this enemy's bitter need for revenge and justify the use of force in retaliation. An implicit link (as distinct from the overt link mentioned above): teaching a child to swim by ultimatum (sink or swim) and bombing a country into seeing reason. Other examples in this chapter include the use of tanks and half-tracks to bring "law and order" to Ilium: in the name of justice, Sodom and Gomorrah are destroyed.

FATHER/MOTHER WORLDS

Violence in the name of social justice exemplifies the attitude of the Father World, as we have seen. So do the "logical" emphasis on rank and the "logical" treatment of cripples that we experience in this chapter. While hundreds of underlings must struggle through wartime conditions without the benefit of female companionship, the German colonel can publicly flaunt one of his privileges: his woman. (Some visitors to Valley Forge are impressed with the difference between the soldier's huts, which packed four lonely men to a tiny room, and the Commanding General's mansion, where he enjoyed the company of his wife.) Seeing the cripples begging at his doorstep, Billy remembers the "objective" information supplied by the Better Business Bureau and does not answer his bell. He weeps and does not know why. The demands of the Father World are harsh: the tears belong to the Mother World and must be hidden and denied. Yet the humane attitudes of the Great Mother keep asserting themselves: when the Germans capture Billy, they dust the snow off his coat; and Billy sees, in the face an enemy soldier, the face of a "blond angel." Notice the sex of the angel: he is a heavenly androgyne (andro = man, gyne = woman), he has crossed the sex line, he combines the best of the two Worlds. Will he be able to avoid the harsh extremes of the Father World?

MAN VERSUS MACHINES

While tanks bring justice to the ghetto and bombers make the North Vietnamese "see reason," even those machines supposedly used for constructive purposes bring no sense of fulfillment to Billy. His Cadillac insulates him from the ghetto he must drive through; taking a nap, he is surrounded by gadgets. The failure of his gadgetry to solve his basic human need for happiness is symbolized in the scene in which Billy turns on the "Gentle Fingers," his automatic vibrator, so that "he was jiggled as he wept." Billy is trapped in a ludicrous and impotent situation.

MOTIFS AND ALLUSIONS

While emphasizing a few of his themes, Vonnegut renews some of his other motifs with mere suggestions or passing references. The extreme youthfulness of many of the soldiers keeps us reminded of the Children's Crusade. The cupola in the Ilium firehouse (which sounds the noon-day siren) of course brings back the image of Goethe in the cupola of the Church of our Lady. And Vonnegut uses a new literary **allusion**. The "tens of thousands" of "humiliated Americans," flowing over the landscape in long columns, under dismal restraint as prisoners of war - "sighed and moaned." As Billy sees them (with his optical illusions created by his being tossed into the shrubbery) they are silhouetted in an eerie light. They are in Dante's Hell. And it is in chapter 3 that the parallel to *Song of Roland* is completed (see paragraph on "Song of Roland Weary" in analysis of chapter 2).

METAPHORIC LANGUAGE

This chapter proves again Vonnegut's ability to produce a reliable series of memorable metaphors. Perhaps the most unforgettable is his extended comparison of military "mopping up" with post-coital play. The comparison is not far-fetched. Other writers have noticed the sexual zest with which militarists regard war. In Mailer's *The Naked and the Dead*, General Cummings indites a passage in his journal in which an artillery shell is a phallic object passing through a cannon that is a vaginal object. This journal entry is made in the happy afterglow of his having fired a cannon on his visit to the front. And it is a historical fact that General George Patton once wrote that "War is the only place where a man really lives." Several of Vonnegut's superb **similes** in this chapter are remarkable for their sense appeal. The prisoners on the floor of the boxcar create a mosaic of sleepers who nestled like spoons. And when the colonel dying of pneumonia talks, his lungs rattled like greasy paper bags. Note that occasionally Vonnegut resorts to synesthesia, or a deliberate blurring of the senses; once he blends sight, sound, and touch: bright sunlight came crashing in.

CHARACTERIZATION

Vonnegut continues to produce rapid but vivid sketches of characters whom we meet just once while he develops in-depth the personality of Billy. The ex-hobo who keeps reminding his buddies that their present circumstances "ain't bad," by comparison with what hobos normally endure, exemplifies the incredible willingness of the human spirit to out-wait adversity. The colonel who always hoped his men would call him "Wild Bob" exemplifies the pathetic delusions of men at war. Vonnegut catches both these men at that telling moment when they try to console themselves by consoling others.

Vonnegut advances his characterization of Billy by revealing more about the fragmentation of Billy's personality. Billy's fantasy life is now linked to specific, unbearable events in "real" life. The boxcar taking him into captivity becomes a flying saucer taking him to serenity. When he scrambles out of the shrubbery where the Germans tossed him, he is living simultaneously in 1944 and 1967. His hallucinations, then, are an escape from the present moment. Sometimes he must also escape from his own past. While the Marine major is talking about the need for bigger and better bombings, Billy "did not shudder about the hideous things he himself had seen bombing do." Here he survives the moment by suppressing his own firsthand knowledge. In private, Billy weeps without knowing why, yet in public he tells the major he is proud of his son in the Green Berets. "I am. I certainly am," he says, in a manner that was long ago identified as "protesting too much." In the next chapter, we shall learn Billy's real answer to the major's advocacy of more bombing. Like the **episodes** reviewed here, it will demonstrate that Billy is torn into fragments: he is a pitiful example of modern man in a society in which the individual must deny his own experience.

SLAUGHTERHOUSE-FIVE

TEXTUAL ANALYSIS

CHAPTER 4

In his fourth chapter, Vonnegut explores the nature and meaning of Billy's fantasies, develops his **themes** of the sterility of modern life and breakdown of communications, and introduces new characters into Billy's story.

BILLY'S FILM FANTASY

Billy's real answer to the major comes in one of the most imaginative and effective scenes of the book, when, unstuck in time again, Billy is actually able to see a TV war-film backward. The result is a perfect wish fulfillment fantasy. Not only do guns suck back the shells they fired and planes retrieve the bombs they dropped, but all military damage to persons and cities is undone, and all materials that made up the weaponry are returned as minerals to the ground whence they were mined. Vonnegut achieves an additional ironic twist near the end of the "film." In wartime, warring nations employ women to make munitions, but in Billy's backward version, it turns out that women are dismantling the ammunition. The greatest **irony** of this scene is that, of course, Billy's fantasy would constitute legal proof of his insanity, while the correct version would not attract much attention as anything except normal TV pap.

STERILITY OF MODERN LIFE

It is significant that Billy's "schizophrenic" version of a World War II movie should be immediately followed by a flight on a flying saucer. Both **episodes** are in the same vein of escape fantasy. In the war-film-run-backward, Billy is denying his knowledge of Dresden. What is he running away from as he takes off in the flying saucer? The answer is partly in the quality of his environment. The champagne is stale, a bottle of soft drink boasts on its label that it contains absolutely no nourishment, Billy's wife (we learn) has had her reproductive organs removed, and Billy's feet are "ivory and blue," a description used of corpses in the combat scenes. These are all symbols of sterility and stasis. Furthermore, the tent in which Billy's daughter was married in Billy's backyard is striped orange and black and Billy and his wife have nestled in their bed like spoons. We know the meaning of this in Billy's experience: a prisoner-of-war-train was marked orange and black and the prisoners in the car slept that way. Billy is a prisoner in civilian life too and in his space flight he is escaping the prison of a sterile life. Note that the pattern is similar to what we found in the preceding chapter: at different times, Billy denies both his past experience and his present situation.

We might ask, why this especially rich fantasy life on the night of his daughter's wedding? There is nothing like a wedding or a birth or a death to make a man take inventory of his own life.

Is his daughter about to enter the sterile prison of conformity that Billy is in? We know she is: we have already met Barbara (later in time, after the marriage, after Valencia's death) and we know that in chapter 2 she served as the perfect expression of bourgeois conformity. So the occasion of her wedding could serve as a reminder to Billy that these sterile patterns of life are about to be repeated, and could trigger off these wish-fulfillment episodes.

MATERIALS FOR TRALFAMADORE EPISODE

We are now able to see how Billy constructs his "space-ship" fantasy out of the materials of his own life. Billy has been watching airships in a war-film, thinking by association about an orange-and-black boxcar that took him into captivity. He has witnessed one more failure in human communication: the "wrong-number" on the telephone. In his office, Billy has a paperweight: a block of amber with three ladybugs embedded in it. Now in his fantasy a spaceship is taking him into captivity; his captors succeed perfectly in communication with him: they go beyond telephony to telepathy. And they explain his (and their) predicament to him: "... here we are, Mr. Pilgrim, trapped in the amber of this moment."

MEANING OF TRALFAMADORE?

We are now in a better position to consider this question. Tralfamadore, its spaceships, and its people are the dream-components with which Billy is working out a mythology to explain the ultimate reality and his place in it. It is no more "fantastic" than any other use of mythology for metaphysical, cosmological, and etiological questions (questions about the nature and origins of reality). Consider, for example, Plato's use of his *Myth of the Cave* to "explain" (i.e., illustrate) the difference between the reality we perceive and the ultimate reality imperceptible to man. Note that Claude Lévi-Strauss, in his various works on mythology, finds mythologizing a mode of thought that resolves contradictions. The psychoanalytic theories of mythology (as propounded by Sigmund Freud, C. G. Jung, and Erich Fromm) explain mythologizing as a dream-process, which employs the basic symbolistic techniques man uses in his dreaming. In his profoundest thinking, in which he uses the "forgotten language" of dream-symbolism, Billy is grappling with the dread questions of free will and the structure of reality. When the Tralfamadorians explain to Billy that we are all bugs trapped in amber, that the moment is structured just the way it has to be, this is the "unconscious" part of Billy's own psyche explaining to the "conscious" part. The net effect is to give Billy perspective: to see time arranged in space. The **simile** used here - "seeing all time as you might see a stretch of the Rocky Mountains" - is the perfect literary expression of the idea because everyone has an image (either from photographs or from air travel over the Rockies) that includes tall individual peaks that nevertheless lose their tallness in the great breadth of the range. This may be a philosophy of resignation, but at least it represents Billy's effort to unify his personality and to come to terms with the seeming absurdity of life.

NARRATIVE, AUTOBIOGRAPHY, AND STERILITY

Vonnegut continues to unravel his story by spiraling back and forth over time, ranging from Billy's infancy far into his golf-playing future. But it becomes obvious by now that on the chronological level, it's the war experiences that structure the novel. Notice that again Vonnegut takes pains to destroy what we would normally call suspense, which an author normally achieves by withholding information about the future. As soon as we meet Edgar Derby, we are told he will die in 68 days. Vonnegut eschews linear time so far as that can be done in a medium committed to cumulative experience. He views all time simultaneously, as from the fourth dimension or as in the dream world. The story is again an amalgam of Vonnegut fact and Pilgrim fiction. The description early in the chapter, of Billy's sense of loneliness in a house with empty children's rooms (they are "children no more ... gone forever"), corresponds to statements Vonnegut made in 1970 when he explained why he had to get away from his Cape Cod house for a while. And of course, the verisimilitude of the description of the prison camp is a direct result of Vonnegut's own POW experience. Note also the juxtaposition of facts separated in time which helps give the novel its fourth-dimensional character. Derby's execution reminds us of Slovik's. The condition of the male genitalia in the shower room (reproduction was not their business) balances the mention early in the chapter of Mrs. Pilgrim's loss of her reproductive organs. These **episodes** are separated by more than 20 years in chronological time; here they are juxtaposed in time synthesis to emphasize a pervasive quality of modern life: sterility.

DESCRIPTION

This fourth chapter illustrates Vonnegut's descriptive power and his virtuosity in description. The prisoner-of-war camp with its minimal lighting, its hellish interiors, and its construction strictly for herding around of human cattle, is unforgettable. The description of the film run backward shows what Vonnegut can do with vocabulary. At that point in the summary of the film where the reader is well aware of what's happening, Vonnegut ceases to identify equipment by its usual names (shells, bullets) and begins to describe it the way an extra-terrestrial being would: anti-air-craft guns are now seen as "long steel tubes" and shells become "cylindrical steel containers." This adds to the "unreality" of the scene and yet forces us to take a fresh look at what is usually regarded as "reality."

SYMBOLISM

Again, a chapter is rich in figures of speech (which helps explain why there is so much compacted into such a "small" book). The prisoner's being issued coats pell-mell and willy-nilly serves here to symbolize the reduction of individuals to interchangeable parts in wartime. The exchanging of shoes and boots (which killed Roland Weary) served the same symbolic function earlier. To this symbolism must also be added the function of the Rocky Mountains, the bugs in amber, and the symbols of sterility, communication, and imprisonment that we mentioned earlier.

CHARACTERIZATION

Billy's characterization has been advanced in terms of his fantasies (discussed above) and in succinct symbolism (he is the only prisoner given a civilian coat!). We should finally note the way in which Vonnegut characterizes the broken spirit of the prisoner. They no longer possess the combination of flexibility and structure, of flesh and bone, that human beings normally have. They are now either rigid as stone (like the dead hobo) or brittle as glass (like Billy, afraid to jump for that reason), or absolutely fluid (like most of the men) and subject to laws of fluid dynamics.

SLAUGHTERHOUSE-FIVE

TEXTUAL ANALYSIS

CHAPTER 5

By now it is clear that Vonnegut is constructing Billy's story out of three strands of material. The author uses Billy's wartime-experiences as the core of the narrative, around which he weaves Billy's peace-time experiences, both pre- and post-war, and his fantasy life, both his "normal" one-time dreams and his serial-dream about Tralfamadore. Going from one strand to another allows Vonnegut now to satirize our society on the realistic level, then to achieve perspective on a fantasy level.

SATIRE ON MODERN WAR

The war scenes are so ghastly in their essence that they could be approached no other way except through **black humor**: the literary approach that makes us laugh so that we shall not cry. The British prisoners typify the way - in wartime - civilized man turns his back on all his "progress" and becomes a scavenger. The fifty British officers are fifty modern Robinson Crusoes, pathetically ingenious in their use of scrap materials and forced to be smug about mere survival. That their esprit delights the Germans is a deft touch of **irony**: the British with their incredible morale actually make war seem "reasonable and fun." They have earned the dubious distinction of being admired by the world's greatest militarists. Vonnegut undercuts the apparent physical and psychological superiority of the British prisoners by making it traceable to a clerical error that results in their getting not 50 but 500 Red Cross parcels and puts them in an ironic bargaining position with their alleged enemy. Notice that as usual, Vonnegut achieves as many balances as possible to show that no one has a monopoly on good or evil. The Germans committed the atrocity of rendering enemies of the state into fat for candles and soap. The Americans, "proud of fighting pure evil," retaliated by boiling schoolgirls alive in a water tower as part of the great fire-raid in Dresden. War reduces the self-righteous avenger of evil to the moral level of his enemy.

SATIRE ON MIDDLE-CLASS MYTHOLOGY

The peacetime scenes begin to add up to a systematic **satire** on American middle-class culture. Vonnegut uses fictitious literary works by characters imported from other novels to expose the hypocrisy in American religious and social values. Of course a visitor from outer space would wonder why Christians find it so easy to be cruel: after all, the basic intent of Gospel preaching, every Sunday, in church and on TV, is to teach people to be merciful even to the lowest of the low. The spaceman's conclusion is apparently fantastic but it accords with the simple Wittgenstein principle that a statement means what it proves to be in practice. The story of the Crucifixion could then in effect mean. "Before you kill anybody, make sure he isn't well connected." And the new Gospel that the spaceman offers is again ironically accurate: for the story of the Crucifixion might have far greater significance if it presented Jesus as a nobody who was then adopted by God as the Son of the Creator. Of course that this spaceman's version does accord with the historical facts as non-believers see them (namely, that an obscure ethical teacher was deified by his followers), adds to the **irony**. American non-religious mythology is also satirized through the "writings of a distant observer, in this case an American who (for very complicated reasons!) has turned Nazi sympathizer and in effect explains American mythology to the Germans. The basic American myth, we infer from his writings, is that it's so easy to make money that anybody who doesn't make money is contemptible. Since the truth is that it's not easy to make money, the American ruling class is spared the responsibility of caring for its poor while the lower classes, brainwashed with this myth, very conveniently learn to hate themselves. Again Vonnegut compounds the **irony** by putting this staggering analysis in a Nazi publication: nobody, we are thus reminded, is totally wrong: if you want perspective on yourself, find out how outsiders view you.

SATIRE ON MARRIAGE AND FAMILY

The American concept of family life continues to take a beating. Love and marriage are reduced to considerations of economic and domestic convenience. This is beautifully satirized in Billy's consummation of his marriage to Valencia: his orgasm is not a **climax** of passion and union with another personality, rather it is the clinching of an economic arrangement. Valencia is not a person, she is a pawn in the patriarchal exchanging of women to preserve the male power-structure. Billy's mother does not love him for his own sake; she loves him in expectation that he will idolize her for her martyrdom. Billy's daughter, Barbara, has learned the bourgeois pattern well: she takes away his dignity in the name of love.

SATIRE OF PSYCHOANALYSIS

In this chapter American psychoanalysis is represented as a tool of middle-class hypocrisy. The doctors explain Billy's post-war breakdown in terms of his relations with his father, not in terms of the horrors of his war service. The Wilhelm Reichian connection between the patriarchal ultimatum (sink-or-swim) and military tyranny is one that the veterans' hospital psychiatrist does not dare to make. War is a "normal" activity, and if the ward is full of veterans who have cracked up, it's their peace-time experience only that has caused it! This is superbly ramified in the community's attitude toward Billy's son: he is a problem in his teens but he straightens out when he becomes a member of the Green Berets! Juvenile delinquency at home is "sick," but extermination abroad is "healthy"!

TRALFAMADORIAN PERSPECTIVE

Vonnegut continues to use Tralfamadore as a stage for speculation about alternatives. What does it mean for Earthlings that the Tralfamadorians recognize five sexes on their planet and seven on Earth? This seems to be a **satire** on the Earthling view toward sexual differences. According to this view, which is patriarchal in nature, masculinity expresses itself in action, logic, social power, and organization; femininity expresses itself in passivity, submission, emotions, and esthetic and domestic matters. In recognizing five to seven sexes as being essential to reproduction, Tralfamadorians seem to be saying that this assignment of qualities according to two sexes is artificial and arbitrary, that human beings have to be free to combine human qualities in more than just two prescribed ways, and that this freedom is essential to continuation of the race. Men should be able to express "feminine" feelings, women to explore their logical powers, in a great variety of combinations. Why, for example, should Billy be forced to weep in private over the "masculine" destruction of Dresden? Why can't weeping be considered a natural masculine prerogative, instead of a sign of unmanliness? The Tralfamadorian view toward war is less instructive. They seem to accept it as universal and inevitable. Billy seems to use his Tralfamadore fantasies in two ways: to explore alternatives to the Earthling view (as on sexuality) and to come to terms with Earthling practice (as in war).

VONNEGUT'S ESTHETICS

The Tralfamadorian concept of literature, certainly, does not represent acceptance of the popular view of Earth. Billy is intelligent and sensitive enough to feel that a best-seller like Jacqueline Susann's *Valley of the Dolls* does not get to the heart of human experience. It is simply an external, "realistic" reporting of "ups and downs" of human experience, ostensibly discovering cause and effect in that experience. Tralfamadorian novels, on the other hand, present a "clump" of images, apparently unrelated but all carefully chosen by the author, so that they represent "the depths of many marvelous moments seen all at one time." We recognize this at once as a description of exactly what Vonnegut himself is attempting in the manner and matter of *Slaughterhouse-Five*. It's easier on the reader, though, in Tralfamadore, where their fourth-dimension perception makes simultaneity of past, present, and future a reality. The Vonnegut esthetic, as we can infer it from this chapter, seems to be:

The function of art is not to reassure man about "meaning" or "purpose" but to enhance our sense of existence, to help us realize our own Selfhood and our unity with reality.

NARRATIVE LINKS

The psychological linkage between the various images is especially ingenious in this chapter: for example, it is Billy's turning on the light that results in his moving from one time-place to another. And of course his waking to discover he has had a "wet dream" is surest proof yet that the Tralfamadorian **episodes** are intended merely as wish-fulfillment fantasies. Notice that the impossibility of escape from Tralfamadore is the dream equivalent of the impossibility of escape from the British compound.

AUTOBIOGRAPHY AND REAPPEARANCE

The works of Kilgore Trout, to which ex-Captain Rosewater introduces Billy, are of course parodies of Vonnegut's own science fiction. Trout's fate-to be ridiculed as a poor writer, to go from publisher to publisher, to suffer obscurity - is not too much an exaggeration of Vonnegut's own fate say from 1952 to 1962. Both Trout and Rosewater, of course, are characters out of *God Bless You, Mr. Rosewater*, and Howard Campbell, Jr., whose propaganda writings for the Nazis contain such shrewd analysis of American mythology, is reincarnated from *Mother Night*. The advantage of these re-appearances is that for regular Vonnegut readers these are not minor characters but legendary figures of long standing; but even the new reader, enjoying his first Vonnegut novel, benefits from the fact that these characters enter this novel full-grown.

STYLE

Again Vonnegut displays great skill in adapting language to situation. The fantastic jollity of the British officers is largely expressed in the vocabulary of the scene which surprises us with words like lusty, ruddy, boomingly, rodomontades, azure curtains, darling elves. Again, describing Derby's capture, Vonnegut pulls back from that level of reality in which we talk of bullets to the level in which we see lumps of lead in copper jackets. A sky full of shrapnel becomes the incredible artificial weather that Earthlings sometimes create for other Earthlings. The effect of course is to make us see familiar things in an unfamiliar way.

CHARACTERIZATION

Several of the minor characters in this chapter have already been mentioned in passing for their chief characteristics: Billy's mother is a caricature of the self-righteous, self-martyring middle-class mother; Valencia is the boss' daughter whose sex is used to ensure continuity of the family business; and the English officers are caricatures of that military attitude toward "morale" which has also been satirized in the movie *The Bridge over the River Kwai*. Eliot Rosewater is still the "type" of the man always inventing a new self but trying-like the hobo-always to console others unselfishly. Montana Wildhack is a (man's) pure wish-fulfillment fantasy: a movie star marooned with one poor awkward unhandsome male to whom she must ultimately turn for love!

Billy's character is more fully developed so that now we are able to make a surprising observation: in wartime, under military circumstances, Billy is a mere victim, willy-nilly a clown. But in peacetime, he is not so stultified. He has good instincts about literature and he can parry well in a difficult conversation about his war experience: “It would sound like a dream. Other people’s dreams aren’t very interesting, usually.” Nevertheless, even the pressures of peace-time life have widened the split in Billy’s personality. His Id shrinks from the very thought of marrying Valencia; his Ego tells him it means success in business. On the social level, his Ego has won; but on the unconscious level, his Id lives on Tralfamadore or among the giraffes. His giraffe dream is a poignant fantasy: tall and spindly, Billy is considered awkward in our society; but among the giraffes of his dream-world he is accepted. Again, the dream world is the more humane: it is the Mother World of pre-patriarchal times for which the human spirit still yearns.

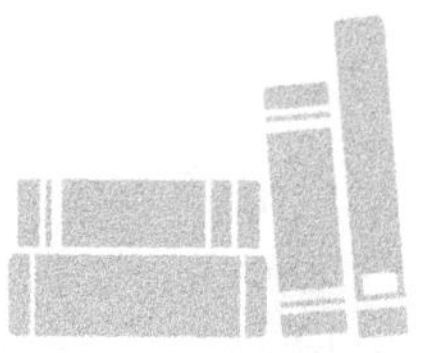

SLAUGHTERHOUSE-FIVE

TEXTUAL ANALYSIS

CHAPTER 6

The chapter just discussed - the fifth - is the longest and most complex chapter in the novel. Now we come to the shortest and simplest chapter so far. Most of the action is on the realistic level with only one fantasy scene. The contrast is effective: it helps create a sense of expectation.

THEMES AND MOTIFS

The sixth chapter abounds in quiet ironies about national pride and international relations.

PATRIOTIC IDEALISM

The basic **irony** of the book is expressed by the British colonel, in his speech to the prisoners, and by the American teacher, Edgar Derby, as he composes a letter to his wife. Both of them emphasize that Dresden will not be bombed because it is an open city. Neither of these two gentlemen could contemplates for one moment that his country could commit such an atrocity, such a violation of international law and human decency. Both gentlemen have entered into this protracted suffering called warfare because they believe their country is on the side of righteousness, committed to punishing international crimes committed by the enemy.

REVENGE THEME

In the same chapter, the whole question of lex talionis (law of retaliation: an eye for an eye) is brought to a quiet, double crisis in the mind of Billy Pilgrim. Notice that Paul Lazzaro's threat to avenge the death of Roland Weary triggers off a fantasy in which Billy extends the consequences of revenge from the personal level to the international level. The dream equation works like this: if Billy is going to be killed for (allegedly) causing Weary's death, then the United States would be divided up into 20 countries so that it could never again be a threat to world peace. Note to the **irony** of the date that Billy dreams up for this scene: Lazzaro will shoot him in 1976, the bicentennial of American Independence. Note finally that this fantasy of the Balkanization of his country is Billy's second answer to the Marine major (the first being the war-film-run-backward) on the fantasy level. (Vonnegut calls such retaliatory division of a country "Balkanization" because for a long time it was the custom of European diplomats to partition countries in the Balkan area so that the fragmented nationalities could not pose much of a threat to peace and theoretically could serve as "buffers" between the big powers. In this sense, Germany was "Balkanized," soon after the wartime action of *Slaughterhouse-Five*, into East Germany and West Germany.)

INTERNATIONAL RELATIONS: MAN TO MAN

These **themes** of the ironies of patriotism and international affairs are reinforced in three little tragicomic scenes: the sudden exclusiveness of the British prisoners; the ominous anxiety of the eight German guards as they go to meet the 100 Americans; and the indignation of the German surgeon that Billy does not take war more seriously. We are left in doubt about the real reason for the British withdrawal from association with the Americans. The Britons' new behavior is in dramatic contrast to their warm welcome the night the "Yanks" arrived. Then we recall that the British officers had been under the delusion that the Americans would also be officers. Instead 100 privates have arrived. After their initial expression of interest in the Americans as human beings, the British have apparently realized that military protocol requires that the officers' area be "off limits" to enlisted men! Notice the strong contrast in the situation with the German guards, an odd squad of under-age and over-age soldiers. They feel nervous about guarding these fierce Americans fresh from combat - until they see them! Then they realize that the Americans are "more fools like themselves," and they relax! Basic humanity expresses itself naturally in this scene between two peoples at war, in contrast to the setting up of artificial barriers of rank in the scene between two peoples who are allied.

CONTRAST AND SUSPENSE

Contrast figures too in Vonnegut's distinction between German cities already bombed, because they are military targets, and the beautiful city of Dresden, "safe" because it is an "open city." But the question poses itself: hasn't Vonnegut destroyed suspense by repeatedly reminding us that Dresden would be wiped out?

The answer is no, in a certain sense, he has actually increased the suspense because he has intensified the dramatic irony. As readers of this chapter, we are in the same position that the Greek theatre-goer was in when he witnessed Oedipus Tyrannos or any other play. He knew the myth already: for him the **irony** was increased because he was watching how the characters acted in their ignorance of the way their fate was going to work out. To us, the "dignity" of the German surgeon, the anxiety of the eight guards, the patriotic idealism of Edgar Derby are all the more poignant because Vonnegut has told us the fate of each in advance.

CHARACTERIZATION

Paul Lazzaro proves in this chapter to be the ugly incarnation of the spirit of revenge. Billy, in his fantasy of public acceptance of death at Lazzaro's hands, is the incarnation of the spirit of pacifism. Billy appears in the military situation to be a fool, but like the official jester in Renaissance drama, he has wisdom and insight behind all the nonsense. His two fantasy-answers to the Marine major show that in some ways, Billy understands the nature of things better than the urbane English colonel does, or the American teacher of international relations.

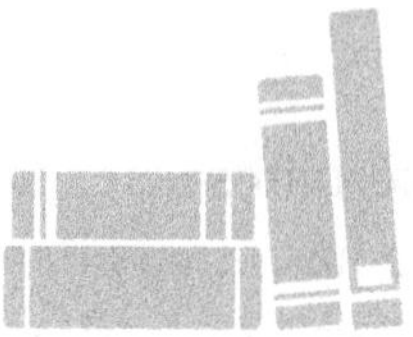

SLAUGHTERHOUSE-FIVE

TEXTUAL ANALYSIS

CHAPTER 7

QUIET APPREHENSION

There are no Tralfamadorian **episodes** at all in the seventh chapter. As though to emphasize the way time-content shrinks without "far-out" fantasy, Vonnegut makes this the shortest chapter so far. The effect again is of quiet expectation. Knowing as we do that Dresden is doomed, in its last 72 hours or so, we slow down and take a good look at everything and everybody. What we see and hear, once again, are the ironies of nationalism.

TWO INTERNATIONAL SITUATIONS

Vonnegut exploits the unusual situation created by the presence of American prisoners of war assigned to work in a German civilian enterprise: both the prisoners and their captors are forced to relate to each other in an "everyday" manner. The overall impression we get of their feelings is a kind of mutual embarrassment at the absurd artificiality (and futility) of it all. Vonnegut compounds the ironies by having Billy recall these Dresden days from a point-in-time 25 years later. The locale is Vermont and the foreign visitors in this contrapuntal situation are Austrian ski-instructors. Note the many balancings, echoes, and contrasts that this double situation provides:

CONTRASTS AND ECHOES

The Americans in Dresden are foreigners experiencing the punishments of war: captivity, humiliation, insecurity, limited opportunities for communication and movement. The Austrians in Vermont are foreigners enjoying the benefits of peace: the dignity of constructive work, free communication (they are teachers), humanitarian activities (rescue work), and dramatic freedom of movement. The optometrist's quartet sings vulgar, naughty-boy, chauvinistic songs about "Polacks," and Billy remembers how back in Dresden he saw a Pole hanged by the Nazis for the capital offense of having sexual relations with an "Aryan" woman. To Billy's sensitive mind, the "innocent" chauvinism of his father-in-law is thus, by free-association, equated with extreme racist doctrine: they are simply different degrees of smug, self-righteous belief in racial supremacy. Note, by contrast, the German war widow who has every human reason to experience bitterness over the presence of enemy soldiers. Yet her basic humanity asserts itself and she inquires as sympathetically about Derby's age as she does about the German boy-soldier's age. The thirty girls - whom the boy-soldier and his prisoners inadvertently see taking showers- strike both an echo and a foreboding in our minds of an incident we know must soon occur: the boiling alive of girls in a water tower. We realize also that this could be young Werner Gluck's last (as well as his first) glimpse of naked women. Modern war destroys the innocent and untested along with the guilty and the jaded.

SYMBOLISM OF THE SYRUP

The ultimate **irony** of this chapter is in the nutritional syrup that is made in the factory to which the American prisoners are assigned. It is formulated for pregnant women - for the nurture of life - and it symbolizes the concerns of the Mother World. And surreptitiously all the men - Germans and their enemies - steal the syrup a spoonful at a time. We have an unforgettable image of Derby, tasting the syrup, with tears forming in his eyes. But soon the concerns of the Father World will destroy the syrup too.

STYLE

The writing is quiet and subdued, but it lives up to the highest demands of the Tralfamadorian esthetic: through a series of carefully chosen images, it enhances our sense of the human predicament.

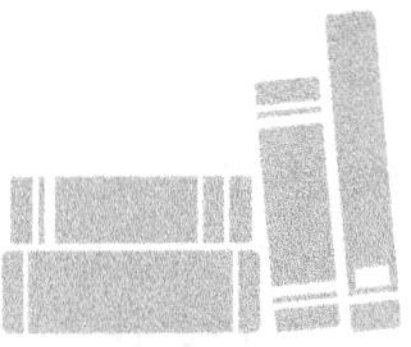

SLAUGHTERHOUSE-FIVE

TEXTUAL ANALYSIS

CHAPTER 8

The eighth chapter develops on all three levels - Billy's wartime experience, his peacetime experience, and his Tralfamadorian fantasy-life-and all of them are concerned with the fire-storm at Dresden.

POINT OF VIEW AND "INDIRECTION"

In this novel, Vonnegut has adopted the point-of-view of the author omniscient. He has been privileged therefore to be inside or above the action as he sees fit. This point-of-view has made it possible for him to go beyond the limits of his main character's perception and to tell us what else is happening anywhere, anytime, and what other characters are thinking. Therefore in handling the actual fire-bombing of Dresden, Vonnegut could have provided us with an overall view of the raid as seen from the air or from some vantage point on the ground. Instead he prefers at this point to limit himself to his main character's perception. The actual bombing is described to us as it is experienced from inside the underground shelter where Billy, his fellow prisoners and guards, spend the hours of the raid.

Now this "strategy ... of indirection" has provided the most serious grounds for adverse criticism of the novel, as we shall see in greater detail later ("Critics Respond to *Slaughterhouse-Five*"). Alfred Kazin, for example, points out that the French author Celine, who was not in Dresden, "tells us more what the Dresden fire-bombing was like than does Vonnegut, who was there ..." Kazin sees Celine's "graphic" description as related to his ability to be outraged by the **episode**, and Vonnegut's "evasion of any realistic description" as related to his failure to "take sides," to judge and condemn. A more sympathetic critic, Father Ernest W. Ranly, wrote that "Vonnegut cannot (nor can any human) face directly evils so incomprehensible as the fire-bombing of Dresden."

IN DEFENSE OF VONNEGUT'S STRATEGY

It seems to us that Kazin's criticism is based on extrinsic considerations and unfair expectations. No author is obliged to be realistic and documentary, and it clearly is not Vonnegut's artistic intention to be realistic. His entire approach, for eight chapters, has been suggestive and psychological. Furthermore, his main purpose has been to study the effect of war (especially of atrocities like Dresden) on people. Billy has been characterized throughout as a man who has managed to survive by avoiding direct contemplation of the horrors around him. In this very chapter, Vonnegut says "One of the main effects of war ... is that people are discouraged from being characters."

EFFECTIVENESS OF INDIRECTION

All of this annoyance with Vonnegut's failure to be photographic overlooks the main question: just how artistically effective is Vonnegut's strategy of indirection? We think that both phases of his description of the raid accomplish their artistic purpose with extraordinary effectiveness. In phase one, we are kept in suspense as we hear "sounds like giant foot-steps above ... The giants walked and walked." We hear a guard, who occasionally looks out, whisper that Dresden is "one big flame." In phase two, when Billy and his guards go outside, we see the results of the flame. The images are few but powerful. People who had been caught in the firestorm are now "little logs lying around." Tall buildings that "used to form cliffs" are now "low and graceful curves" of rubble. There was nothing but "ashes and dollops of melted glass," it was "like the moon," and the prisoners and guards become an expedition crossing that desolate, lifeless satellite. Two final images complete the horror for us. American planes come in "under the smoke to see if anything was moving," and they kill some people who survived by the riverside. The prisoners find, on the outskirts of Dresden, an inn where the tables are set for supper and the waiters are waiting but no guests arrive. This suggestive, indirect, economical way of handling the atrocity leaves the rest to the imagination, which means that the horror can remain unbelievable and infinite. A documentary, photographically "realistic" account would allow the reader to contain and dominate the situation and hence it would become finite and believable after all.

VONNEGUT'S JUDGMENT

Vonnegut's judgment of the immorality of the raid is also delivered by indirection, but it is there for any imaginative reader to experience. For example, in this very chapter, we are given a summary of Kilgore Trout's science-fiction novel, *The Gutless Wonder*. A robot-pilot drops burning jellied gasoline on human beings. Nobody holds it against him that he drops jellied gasoline on people, but they find his halitosis unforgivable. Once he clears that up, he is welcomed to the human race. This is an imaginative and effective judgment of both the military and the civilian minds that can connive at atrocities: for it says that anybody who can commit them must be a robot in the first place, and it satirizes the strange system of values that can accept these robots as people. But Kazin, unfortunately, considers science fiction a "boy's fantasy" and so, not having the advantages of a boy's fresh imagination, he misses the point. There are other expressions of Vonnegut's "judgment" of the raid and the "mind" that planned and executed it, but none of them shapes up like the expression of moral indignation that Kazin and numerous other critics expected. They missed the point here too. If Vonnegut were to deliver a moral diatribe against the Dresden atrocity-makers, he would have to assume the same kind of self-righteousness that made the raid possible in the first place.

AUTOBIOGRAPHICAL ELEMENTS

This chapter is highly autobiographical in several ways. Vonnegut himself was in that shelter, under the walking giants, and he himself took that moon-walk. And eighteen years later Vonnegut's situation was much like that of Kilgore Trout who appears in person at Billy Pilgrim's eighteenth wedding-anniversary party: Vonnegut was author of numerous stories but still unrecognized as a writer, except for a small diverse following of underground literati and science-fiction fans. Like Trout, who "makes up a story" spontaneously in the course of party conversation, Vonnegut had once spontaneously created the basic situation for a novel (*The Sirens of Titan*) in casual party-chatter with an editor.

REAPPEARANCE: TWO SIDES OF CAMPBELL

Kilgore Trout, of course, is a reincarnation of the science-fiction writer who helps resolve Eliot Rosewater's situation in *God Bless You, Mr. Rosewater*. And Howard W. Campbell, Jr., first appeared as the main character of *Mother Night*. Vonnegut uses a different point of view this time, however. In *Mother Night*, we saw both the public side of Campbell (he was apparently an active Nazi sympathizer and a traitor to America) and the private, secret side (in "actuality," he was an American spy). But now in *Slaughterhouse-Five* Vonnegut shows us only the public side. The moral question, of course, is this: does Campbell do more damage to America in his public role than he does good in his secret role? Vonnegut said, in a special preface to the 1966 re-issue of *Mother Night*, that we are what we pretend to be.

CHARACTERIZATION

Vonnegut reminds us in this chapter why he cannot tell a traditional realistic story, with "characters" and "dramatic confrontations": "enormous" forces like modern warfare "discourage" people from being characters. This is part of his ironic tribute to Edgar Derby, who stands up to Campbell's defamation of America: America, asserts Derby, believes in fair play, and Derby believes in it too. The **irony**, of course, consists in the fact that Derby's patriotic belief includes the assumption that America will never bomb an open city. Still Derby's patriotism is a far finer thing than Campbell's in this scene. In spite of Americans who are about to betray Derby's beliefs, the direction of Derby's Americanism is toward a better world. Campbell, even in his uniform, is exploiting American traditions for the fuel they might give to fascism. This **irony** is more explicit in his shoulder-patch: Lincoln's profile. Hitler's racism is the diametric opposite of Lincoln's humanitarianism, but if exploiting Americans' pride in Lincoln will attract them to a Nazi crusade, the Nazis are willing to "glorify" Lincoln. Vonnegut's caricature of American fascism in this scene typifies his wariness about the uses to which any "glorified ideal" can be put. There are too many people who accept the "ideal" uncritically. Perhaps it's the function of Maggie White in this chapter to illustrate this: she really believes that advertisers must tell the truth or they'll get in trouble. Notice how ironically Kilgore Trout probes into her other beliefs: in torture in the hereafter, for example.

Billy Pilgrim is represented in this chapter as coming closer to grips with himself, as beginning to undo the denial of his own experience that has typified so much of his behavior. Usually he escapes the consequences of any remote reminder of Dresden or capture in Luxembourg. Today he deliberately concentrates on his "grotesque" reaction to the quartet and its song: he forces his conscious mind to face the facts it has repressed into his "unconscious, and he succeeds. The night of the Dresden raid he had commented to himself that the guards looked like a barbershop quartet. Thanks to Billy's new courage, we have the account of the Dresden raid as he experienced it. Billy is coming closer to "secrets from himself." This has already been symbolized in his successful search for and association with Kilgore Trout, whose interests in the "fourth-dimension" include "time warps and extrasensory perception and other unexpected things" and who, of course, described atrocity-making aviators as robots.

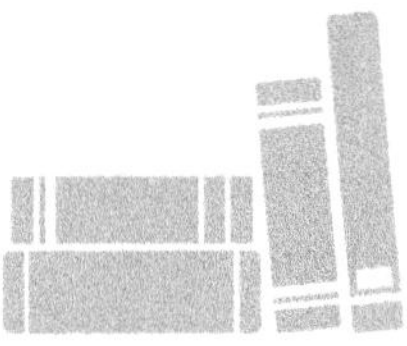

SLAUGHTERHOUSE-FIVE

TEXTUAL ANALYSIS

CHAPTER 9

In his ninth chapter, Vonnegut continues his attack (directly now as well as indirectly) on war, the military mind, and self-righteousness; he continues to be concerned with the breakdown of communications and with man and his machines; he more clearly links Billy Pilgrim with Jesus and more directly acknowledges the linkage between Billy's fantasy life and "real" life.

COMMUNICATIONS

The breakdown in communications is symbolized in Lily's pretending she can read President Truman's justification of the atom-bombing of Hiroshima and in Professor Rumfoord's insisting that everything Billy says about Dresden is part of a "sickness." On the broader national level, the people at large are kept ignorant of Dresden by the technique of de-emphasis: the

27-volume official history of air operations in World II gives the Dresden raid very little attention.

WAR AND SELF-RIGHTEOUSNESS

One thing Lily misses - and probably most readers also missed at the time - is the defensive tone of the Truman message on Hiroshima (as well as its unacknowledged implications for the Dresden raid). The Japanese began the war from the air and now they have been repaid many-fold. This is the lex talionis **theme** again: if the Japanese are evil in committing an atrocity at Pearl Harbor, we are virtuous in committing an atrocity at Hiroshima. Sodom and Gomorrah are evil; violent destruction of all its people is virtue. Truman emphasized too that Hiroshima was an important Japanese Army base: Dresden has no military base at all. Note Vonnegut's supporting images in the same chapter: when Billy tells Montana he has seen an old "blue movie" of hers, she counters by calling Derby's fate a "blue movie with a firing squad." The equation means that war is as obscene as pornography. Again, when Rumfoord tries to attribute Billy's remarks about Dresden to "echolalia," the author omniscient exercises his privilege of direct comment: he says Rumfoord was thinking in a "military manner," that is, thinking that "an inconvenient person, one whose death he wished for very much, for practical reasons, was suffering from a repulsive disease." Note the equation operating again: Montana shifts their baby from one breast to the other because the "moment was so structured that she had to do so." And Billy agrees finally with Rumfoord that "everybody has to do exactly what he does." Only we - not Rumfoord - know what Billy means when he says "I learned that on Tralfamadore." Tralfamadore is the place where Billy becomes reconciled with the impossible and the incredible.

MAN VERSUS MACHINES

Vonnegut describes in proportionately great detail how Valencia died of carbon-monoxide poisoning after the exhaust system of her car is destroyed in an accident. Note that the description is replete with military allusions: The bumper was at a high port arms ... The Cadillac ... sounded like a heavy bomber coming in on a wing and a prayer. We are reminded now that in chapter 1 Vonnegut gave us a detailed story of the death of a veteran in an elevator accident. Why then does he handle the Dresden violence obliquely? The question seems to answer itself: in detailing two horrible deaths for us but merely suggesting the magnitude of the Dresden holocaust, Vonnegut allows us to imagine what 135,000 simultaneous deaths must have been like.

AUTOBIOGRAPHICAL ELEMENTS: REAPPEARANCE

Note that Vonnegut again identifies Billy Pilgrim as being partly autobiographical in his military experiences at least: in chapter 1 Vonnegut described himself as coming home with a ceremonial Luftwaffe saber; in chapter 9 Billy finds it imbedded in a pole. Professor Rumfoord is a member of the Rumfoord family which figures prominently in *The Sirens of Titan*.

SOURCES OF BILLY'S FANTASIES

In this chapter Vonnegut also links Billy's fantasies to the horrors he experiences: unable to face the double tragedy of his wife's car death and his own airplane accident, Billy contemplates public lectures about the negligibility of death, and that involves both the true nature of time and flying saucers. The real sources of Billy's Tralfamadorian adventures are revealed to us when

Billy discovers a Trout novel in which extraterrestrials put Earthlings in a zoo and sees an old peepshow and old girlie magazines featuring Montana Wildhack. As the novel nears its end, Vonnegut is careful to provide realistic motivation for everything fictitious or fantastic. Only a historical event like Dresden remains unaccounted for.

CHARACTERIZATION

Rumfoord is the kind of chest thumping man that Vonnegut satirizes in *Happy Birthday, Wanda June*. Note that again a marriage is represented as being consummated for extrinsic reasons: this time to provide the aged Rumfoord with public proof of virility. The details about Billy's son Robert are disconcerting. He was a juvenile delinquent but now he's "all straightened out." Vonnegut takes pains to make it clear that Robert is clean on the surface and that's all his society cares about. As time spirals through another generation, we imagine for ourselves how Robert weeps and fantasizes as his delayed reactions to atrocities in Vietnam.

We have already identified Billy Pilgrim with the Christian pilgrimage because of the pointed connection between his name and the novel *Pilgrim's Progress*. Vonnegut has kept the **allusion** alive by saying, in chapter 4, that Billy was "self-crucified" on a corner-brace of the boxcar. Now in chapter 9 he directly relates Billy to the Christ of the Christmas carol, a quatrain of which serves as an epigraph for the novel:

> The cattle are lowing, The baby awakes. But the little Lord Jesus No crying He makes.

This prepares us for another Kilgore Trout story, this one about a time-traveler who has two experiences relevant to our present pilgrim's pilgrimage: he sees the twelve-year old Jesus and his carpenter father, Joseph, accept a contract to build a cross for the execution of a rabble-rouser. The implication here is that no one, not even Jesus, escapes complicity in mankind's evil. The second discovery of the time-traveler is in response to the oft-posed question whether Jesus really died on the cross. (An ancient Hebrew legend told that he had been taken down alive, revived in Joseph's tomb, and carried off into the hills three days later by his followers. This legend forms the basis for George Moore's splendid experimental novel *The Brook Kerith* [1915] as well as for an inferior version published in 1972.) The time-traveler's proof, with a stethoscope, that "The Son of God was dead as a doornail" seems to be Vonnegut's version of a theme common in contemporary literature: God is Dead.

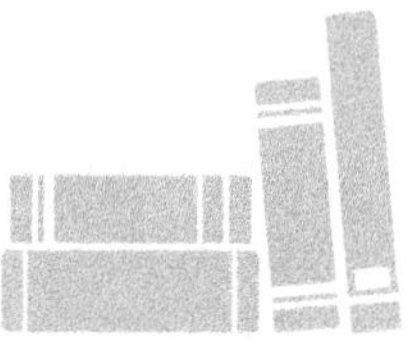

SLAUGHTERHOUSE-FIVE

TEXTUAL ANALYSIS

CHAPTER 10

Vonnegut ends his novel in a restatement of the eternal human predicament: two ways of life exist side by side, death-urge and creative-urge apparently in a race for total control, with comprehension of it all apparently possible only from some remote (Tralfamadorian) perspective. But one thing is different now: art, in its view today as distinct from past views of "eternal truths," no longer promises catharsis, no longer imposes meaning on experience.

TWO WAYS

This chapter presents a constellation of polarities. It begins with contrasting ways of life: destructive "military science" racks up a daily "body-count" in Vietnam while a working artist allows a gun-collection to rust. Opposing urges are revealed again in time-contrasts: a flight over Germany in 1967 does not result in "blackout" below, a Hungarian pilot can smoke Cuban cigars because his government is at peace with Cuba, while the flight does remind at least two people aboard of quite different flights in 1945: the reader recalls the strafing mission, for example. And the chapter ends with a simultaneous view of timeless symbols of death (a coffin-shaped wagon, waiting) and of life (trees leafing out).

METAPHORS

Other figures of speech, more uniquely Vonnegut's, blend in with the conventional symbols and demonstrate again his extraordinary power with **metaphor**. Underground bomb shelters, which contain most of the 135,000 dead, become, in the recovery operation, corpse mines. The dead people, sitting on their benches below their "open city," constitute a wax museum.

DARWIN AND TRALFAMADORE

Vonnegut's **allusion** to Darwin's theory of "natural selection" has an ironic effect here: it is the Tralfamadorians who can so easily apply Darwin's hypothesis to wartime massacre. For in Tralfamadore, where people live all of their life simultaneously and forever, such objectivity and perspective is simple. But in this same chapter, Vonnegut offers hints that maybe the Darwinian view of the function of war no longer applies. According to Darwin, war can be seen as an illustration of the notion that struggle for existence within species among specimens with individual variations results in survival of the fittest. Now in describing the Maori captured at Tobruk, Vonnegut implicitly makes the same point he made about Edgar Derby: here is another good physical specimen in good biological condition. Both Derby and the Maori die in this chapter. Modern warfare does not weed out the unfit and select the fittest for survival. Derby and the Maori are both wiped out as a consequence of war-created conditions that no human being can expect to survive. The 135,000 people in the "corpse mines" - whose massive putrefaction kills the Maori - are uniformly dead without regard to their individual variation.

ART WITHOUT CATHARSIS

In his opening chapter, and again in his scene in which Derby confronts Campbell, Vonnegut implicitly states his opinion of traditional literary form: it does not apply to the human predicament, certainly not to the modern condition of humanity. Traditional literary form pits "characters" into conflict with a definable evil; the form results in "catharsis," which apparently means both a purgation of the emotions (conflicts) engendered by the plot and some kind of insight or comprehension, some recognition of meaning in the action. Traditional art (as Mrs. O'Hare feared in chapter 1) would make Billy Pilgrim into a hero on the side of righteousness, a conscious sufferer who transcends combat with an evil enemy and emerges with some greater wisdom and nobility. But Vonnegut makes it clear: that there is nothing intelligent to be said about a massacre; that when the massacre is committed by your side, you are no longer fighting evil, you are committed to it; that the worst effect of modern war (and maybe even of peacetime technology) is that it squashes people so that they no longer are "characters." In his parable of *The Gutless Wonder*, Vonnegut indicates that such squashed personalities have become robots - maybe still acceptable to the human race but not qualified to be "characters." So *Slaughterhouse-Five* ends without catharsis, without significant character development, with only this measure of progress: at least this conception of art is more truthful and may thus present a new starting point for contemplation of the human predicament.

SLAUGHTERHOUSE-FIVE

CHARACTER ANALYSES

Our analysis will aim to show how each character is an individual force yet contributes to the overall effects of the novel. We shall consider all of the secondary characters in alphabetical order. Since all of them contribute something to Billy's life, we shall thus have a fuller picture of the central character if we consider him last.

SECONDARY CHARACTERS

Campbell, Howard W., Jr.

American writer turned traitor, now serving as propagandist for Hitler, Campbell serves several purposes in the story. First, through Campbell the author can remind us of the ironic fact that we have produced many native American fascists. Secondly, in his uniform and his manner, Campbell is a living **satire** on chauvinism, or patriotism carried to ludicrous, supremacist, racist extremes. Thirdly, Campbell's appeal to the American POWs to fight with the Nazis against the Russians has the effect of motivating Edgar Derby to a really heroic moment. Finally, in his propaganda-writing, Campbell makes incisive criticism of the American ruling-class and the brainwashed poor: thus Vonnegut makes his point that even rabid enemies can hit on truths about us that we ourselves tend to overlook.

So far we have established the function of Campbell as he is known to readers who have met him only in *Slaughterhouse-Five*. But to readers who had previously met him in *Mother Night*, in which Campbell is the main character, his appearance in Billy's story has many additional meanings and connotations. In *Mother Night*, Campbell is an American who publicly appears to be a traitor but who secretly is an American agent. In his propaganda broadcasts for Hitler, he gives coded information to Washington. The **irony** in his situation is that he ultimately learns he did more good for the Nazi cause in his "cover" role than he did for the American cause in his secret role. In a 1966 re-issue of *Mother Night*, Vonnegut said we are what we pretend to be, and so we must be careful about what we pretend to be.

The regular Vonnegut reader, then, sees Campbell in a different light in *Slaughterhouse-Five*. He sees not a real traitor but an agent acting out his role. Perhaps that's why Campbell goes to such extremes in his uniform and manner: he is overacting, perhaps unconsciously, in an effort to prevent the Nazis from being suspicious, or perhaps consciously, so as to be ineffective as a Nazi recruiter. Who knows, at this point, what such an absurdly complicated man is doing, in such an involuted life of sham?

Colonel Of Infantry, "Head Englishman"

A "type" character - the urbane upper-class Englishman - he adds to the characterization, the **Black Humor**, the pathos of war, the

irony of the plot. In his manner and his precept, he stands in stark contrast to the drooping, demoralized Americans. Ironically, the spirited morale that he and his men have maintained has earned the adoration of the Nazis, to whom he serves as proof that war is "reasonable and fun." In his description of Derby he helps to characterize that teacher-soldier, and in nominating Derby to be leader of the Americans, he precipitates a scene in which the indifference of American prisoners that Campbell described is dramatized for us. In confiding that he has not seen a woman or a child, or even a tree, in five years, the Colonel adds a poignant note to the panorama of war. And finally, in his assurance to the Americans that they are going to a safe place, an "open city," that will never be bombed, the Colonel underscores the **irony** of the impending atrocity. It is the colonel's confidence that his country will honor an international law that makes it easy for him to offer such reassurance.

Derby, Edgar

All of the **irony** in Vonnegut's characterization of Derby is summed up in the symbolic occupation that Vonnegut ascribes to him: Derby is by profession a teacher of international relations. He knows that his country would never bomb an open city, and he is able to stand up heroically to Campbell and declare that the United States believes in fair play. But Derby also knows both the rules about looting and the military mind, and still he (absentmindedly?) picks up a teapot among the ruins! His execution as a looter adds to the overall picture of war's horror and absurdity. Note that Derby's standing up to Campbell gives Vonnegut his chance to remark that Derby is practically the only man in the book acting like a character, because "one of the main effects of war is that people are discouraged from being characters." Derby is literally one man in a hundred.

Gluck, Werner

The only one of the eight guards of whom we get a closeup, Werner serves to remind us that the enemy are also human beings; that the enemy too is engaged in a Children's Crusade; that war destroys the fresh and untried, like Werner, along with the seasoned and the knowledgeable, like Derby.

Hobo

Note that the ex-hobo dies as a soldier just the way he lived as a hobo: in horrible unsanitary conditions in a boxcar. Through the brief appearance of this man, Vonnegut demonstrates that war reduces most soldiers to the hour-by-hour anxiety and squalor of the hobo.

Lazzaro, Paul

He plays an important part in Billy's dream-algebra. Even in real life, though, Lazzaro is a nightmarish figure, an ugly incarnation of the spirit of revenge. He is accustomed to taking the law into his own hands, settling all matters through direct physical force. Note the dream-equation in Billy's fantasy-life that is triggered off by Lazzaro's threats: if Lazzaro can kill Billy for allegedly causing Weary's death, then other nations can divide up Billy's country for being a threat to world peace. Lex talionis (law of retaliation) seems as ugly at the international level as it is on Lazzaro's level.

Maori

His ghastly death - caused by inhaling the putrefaction in the "corpse mines" - serves two narrative functions: it shows that even a powerful physical specimen, from a "primitive" tribe, can succumb to the horrors of modern war; it shows how close Billy, who worked by the Maori's side, came to dying from the same exposure.

Merble, Lionel, optometrist, Billy's father-in-law

A chauvinist and a patriarch, his function in the story is to help define Billy's split personality. Merble does this in two ways: (1) His fondness for vulgar songs about "Polacks" triggers off in Billy's mind a free-association that shows, on the unconscious level at least, that Billy is aware that Merble's racist attitudes resemble those of the Nazis. But on the conscious level Billy says nothing, even accepting his politics ready-made from his father-in-law. (2) Merble's use of his optometry business as the bait with which to trap Billy into marrying Miss Merble precipitates Billy's nervous breakdown: on the level of ego-striving, he wants the business, but on the level of physical instinct, he finds Valencia Merble repulsive. Billy's ego defeats his id and Merble secures for himself the blessings of immortality as patriarchy defines it.

O'Hare, Bernard, attorney

He serves mainly as a foil, or a strong contrast to underscore the traits of other characters. For example, in the truckload of prisoners on their way back to the American lines, most of the men are hugging coveted trophies or souvenirs of war. O'Hare is empty-handed. When Vonnegut is enthusiastic about having found the **climax** of his war story, O'Hare seems embarrassed by the writer's efforts to exploit their war experiences. O'Hare, unlike most veterans, has no good war stories to recall. He even tells a white lie in an effort to fend off an argument about war novels between his wife and his friend. O'Hare serves to take all the delusion and phony glamor out of war service.

O'Hare, Mrs. Mary

She performs three important functions in the launching of the story. (1) She introduces the attitudes of the Mother World, in contrast to the attitudes of Jehovah (at Sodom and Gomorrah) and of the ex-colonel at General Electric, who sound the motifs of the Father World. (2) She offers a brilliant explanation of how male writers naively help to make war attractive: when a veteran writes his war novel, he imposes on the immaturity of his days as a boy-soldier all the maturity of the man-writer so that the childish war experiences are imbued with a sense of purpose, dignity, and nobility they did not have in actuality. (3) This prompts Vonnegut to relate his story to the Children's Crusade, apparently (we realize later) by free-association to the English colonel's remarks about the boyishness of the American soldiers.

Pilgrim, Mr.

Billy's father stands for the values of the authoritarian Father World. Smugly, self-righteously, he believes that throwing a mild-mannered, introspective boy into the deep end of a pool will teach him to swim, will shock him into being aggressive. Notice that Billy first becomes "unstuck" in time when he yields to this sink-or-swim experiment, and he is a passive yielder ever after. Under the pretense of showing Billy the wonders of Nature, Mr. Pilgrim can overlook the boy's terror at the edge of the Grand Canyon. Note now the contrast in Billy's being unstuck in time and his father's being anchored in it: Mr. Pilgrim defies the blackness of the deep cavern by taking out his luminous watch. Rather than float on psychological time, he dominates the situation by keeping in touch with mechanical time. The characterization of Father Pilgrim demonstrates the author's ability to create complex creatures with a few deft sketches.

Pilgrim, Mrs.

Billy's mother contributes in at least four ways to the story and the plot. (1) In expecting gratitude from her son, in calling attention to her martyrdom as a mother, she adds to the **satire** on the self-righteousness of middle-class parenthood. (2) Vonnegut's characterization of her indicates that her cannibalistic attitudes toward her son are partly a result of her empty spiritual life, which - again typically bourgeois - she tries to fill with quaint knick-knacks. (3) Her pathetic aging serves to remind Billy of mortality, to increase his need for timeless Tralfamadore. (4) Her putting the gory crucifix on Billy's wall introduces the Jesus **theme** into Billy's story and again symbolizes her reliance on objects instead of on spiritual experience.

Pilgrim, Barbara

Billy's daughter contributes to (1) the **satire** and (2) the plot. (1) She is fact-bound, conventional, more worried about what people will think than about what is really wrong with her father. She seems to feel that his main duty is to keep up appearances. She is delighted to discover how much she can attack him under the guise of "caring" for him. She is a succinct embodiment of middleclass phlegmatism and hypocrisy. (2) Her assaults in the name of love drive him into fantasies about warmer, more genuine intimacy with his consort on Tralfamadore.

Pilgrim, Robert

Billy's son contributes to both (1) the revelation of middle-class values and (2) the progress of Billy's withdrawal. (1) Robert is driven into juvenile delinquency. His knocking over of tombstones is a very symbolic act which literal-minded adults cannot read. No one seems to care about real reasons for his protest against death-in-life: a sterile home environment, a self indulgent, passive glob of a mother, a victim of war-trauma for a father. But as soon as Robert commits mayhem overseas, under official auspices, he is assumed to have developed "character," to have redeemed himself. His polished boots, his natty uniform, symbolize that his development is all external, but outer conformity is all his society wants. (2) Meanwhile Billy, publicly proud over Robert's being "straightened out," weeps indoors without knowing why, withdraws further from reality.

Pilgrim, Valencia Merble, Billy's wife

She is a type, the boss' daughter whose marriageability is a factor in the business scheming of her father. Vonnegut uses her naive conformity as a vehicle for **satire** of middle-class attitudes toward material goods and permanence. Her death-by accidental carbon-monoxide poisoning illustrates the extent to which man is victimized by his own machinery; that this death is precipitated by her hysteria over Billy's airplane crash somewhat redeems her as a character. Her maiden-name is a typical tag-name. It echoes the German word for furniture.

Public Relations Director

He is one of the first representatives of the Father World that we encounter. An ex-lieutenant colonel, even in civilian life he judges people by their ex-military rank, by their willingness to go after rank. He smugly assumes the absolute value of externals and of pushy-ness.

Rumfoord, Prof. Bertram Copeland

Vonnegut introduces him (1) to provide background information on the Establishment's attitude toward the Dresden fire-storm, (2) to underscore Billy's character by contrast, and (3) to further characterize the Father World. (1) Again Vonnegut uses **irony** in plot development. The professor's predicament is that he must condense a 27-volume history of air combat into a one-volume edition, yet include an account of Dresden (because of growing public inquiry) which was largely ignored in the original 27 volumes. This is **black humor**: a condensation of official accounts must reveal information excluded from the "unabridged" version! (2) Rumfoord's attitude about the Dresden raid is the grim opposite of Billy's: Rumfoord can override all humane and legal considerations, saying authoritatively it had to be done (which his own documents gainsay); Billy has been overridden by the event itself, so much so that he represses his own memories of Derby's and the colonel's assurances about an "open city." (3) Rumfoord triumphs over Billy because

Rumfoord is the sink-or-swim father-figure all over again. Billy is preconditioned to sink. Note the likening of Rumfoord to President Theodore Roosevelt, who summed it all up in three proud words: "I took Panama!"

Rumfoord, Lily

She (1) ramifies Vonnegut's **theme** of the breakdown in communications and (2) adds another detail to our view of the Father World. (1) She cannot read well, cannot evaluate the President's announcement of the atom-bomb: she symbolizes the passive public. (2) A gold-digger who sells herself to the elderly rich, she also symbolizes the power of the patriarchy to buy people.

Rosewater, Eliot

He contributes (1) to clearer dramatization of the conflicting values of the Father and Mother Worlds and (2) to Billy's character development. (1) Note that he deliberately experiments with inventing a new self. He once identified with the Father World when he became an Infantry captain. Having killed a fourteen-year-old fireman whom he had taken to be a German soldier, Rosewater finds he has to contend with his humanitarian (Mother World) instincts. This has led him to total revaluation of our culture, as his science-fiction addiction indicates. (2) Rosewater's inducting Billy into the world of "sci-fi" is crucial to Billy's growth. Reading Kilgore Trout's books and then meeting the man himself proves to be Billy's way to self-confrontation.

Again, these remarks reflect what a reader knows who has met the character only in *Slaughterhouse-Five*. For the reader familiar with *God Bless You, Mr. Rosewater*, the man in the hospital bed next to Billy's is not a minor character but a legend. In that book, Rosewater is a rich man who uses his wealth to help people made useless by technological unemployment and other quirks of the System. Naturally, he is considered insane: in the Father World, the normal thing for a man to do with a personal fortune is to try to increase his personal fortune.

Scouts

They represent well-trained soldiers, seriously committed to war. They function almost automatically; they enjoy the exercise of low cunning powered by danger. By contrast they underscore the characters of Roland, officious bustler who manically overdramatizes his part in the action, and Billy, totally incapable of understanding what war is all about. **Irony**: it's the scouts who get killed in these patrol activities.

Trout, Kilgore, science-fiction writer

He has three functions in the development of the action. (1) Trout's earning his living as a news-dealer, unrecognized for his excellent fiction, parodies Vonnegut's own situation in the Fifties, when he was a car-dealer and his books were ignored by literary critics. (2) Trout's various concepts (*The Gutless Wonder*, the new Jesus story, sexual differentiation of Tralfamadore) provide Vonnegut with parables and perspective on our culture and supply the basic mythology for Billy's fantasies. (3) Trout's very presence inspires Billy at last to face his own experience of February 13, 1945.

Vonnegut-The-Character

The author puts himself into chapters 1 and 10 in order to develop his **theme** that art cannot comprehend war and still be honest. We must realize that Vonnegut-the-character is just as much a creation as is any other character. He is based on materials selected from real life in order to make a point for the author. As soon as Vonnegut-the-character is made to face the O'Hares-as-characters, they must all change to fit a pattern that is moving toward a certain revelation. They are all simplified, exaggerated, incomplete, tendentious. It may be true that Vonnegut-the-author was, in real life, as tongue-in-cheek as Vonnegut-the-character is in chapter 1 when he gives O'Hare an outline of his story ("The **irony** is so great"). But when he dramatized that real-life scene, Vonnegut had to use special lighting to get the emphasis he wanted.

War Widow in Dresden

She serves two purposes: she shows that Mother-World concern knows no artificial boundaries of nationality (she is as curious about the American soldiers as she is about Werner Gluck); and in her remark that all the good soldiers are dead, she not only refers to her husband but also reveals the grim fact that the war has reached that final stage where boys and old men are being drafted.

Weary, Roland, antitank-gun crewman

He is important because Vonnegut uses him (1) for a **parody** on a major work of war literature, (2) to illustrate "games people play," and (3) as a foil for Billy. (1) As we have shown in detail in our "Textual Analysis," Roland's last day in combat parallels, step-by-step, the main action of Chanson de Roland (*The Song of Roland*). Through this parallel, Vonnegut makes many contrasts between the "heroic" concept of war and his own. In *The Song of Roland*, it is "Roland, Weary" who is taken by the angels. In *Slaughterhouse-Five*, it is not Roland Weary the sadist but Billy the pacifist who looks up to see the "blond angel." (2) Vonnegut analyzes Roland's habitual neurotic behavior in terms that Eric Berne (*Games People Play*) and R. D. Laing (*The Politics of Experience*) have developed in psychiatry: a person's entire life can be seen as the endless replaying of a basic film-script developed early in his childhood. In Roland's case, he is fearful of being "ditched," so he always seeks out someone less popular than himself, feigns friendship, and at a crucial moment, "ditches" his victim first. In the combat scenes, he has set up this archetypal situation with Billy. **Black Humor**: The scouts ditch him before he can ditch Billy. (3) Roland is a pathetic sadist who enjoys weapons even in civilian life. In his extended fantasy, he is a hero who saved the life of an incompetent "college kid." He underscores by contrast the character of Billy, who is pacifistic and whose fantasies never involve "showing up" anybody but emphasize conquests over his own weaknesses.

White, Maggie

Vonnegut uses her for his **satire** on people who believe everything the Establishment wants them to believe. She doesn't read books but she adores live authors.

"Wild Bob," Infantry colonel

He stands for the pathos and suffering in war, as well as for its delusions. Even as he's dying on his feet, he exhorts "his" troops to think well of their accomplishments. **Black Humor**: "Wild Bob" is the kind of name that admirers give a hero (we think, for example, of General "Mad Anthony" Wayne), but "Wild Bob" has apparently dubbed himself with a name he had hoped would catch on. Clue: Vonnegut tells us the colonel comes from Cody, Wyoming, which could be named after "Wild Bill" Cody, also known as "Buffalo Bill." Vonnegut always gives us the sources of fantasy.

Wildhack, Montana

She plays an important part in Vonnegut's depiction of levels of creation. She has an "objective" existence as a star in "blue movies." She is pictured in "girlie magazines." When Billy in his Tralfamadorian fantasy is about to be mated to an Earthling female, he recreates her from his experience with Montana in pornography. Then Vonnegut uses her as a character in his creation. Why? Apparently to demonstrate what the typical middle-class male, bored in a sterile and prudish marriage, wants as compensation. The fact that it is a better relationship for Billy is made clear in this contrast: Billy cannot tell his wife the full story of Dresden, but he can tell it to Montana. Tag-Name: Montana connotes "hilly." She is a "hack" in the sense that she takes all kinds of odd jobs. Again, note that performers' names are often deliberately coined. Like "Wild Bob," Wildhack could be a self-conceived name. She is a fantasy creation on many levels.

CENTRAL CHARACTER

Billy Pilgrim, optometrist and survivor of Dresden

In creating and developing Billy Pilgrim, Vonnegut's intention is to show the effect of modern war on a sensitive person who tries to play the game the way society expects. But Vonnegut sees he must include two other influences on this person: the effects of family and technology. For the same society that wages massive war fosters the authoritarian family and places machinery above humanity.

Billy is a mild-mannered boy whose father tries to terrify him into a more aggressive way of life. His mother confuses him with her inordinate demands for gratitude. We can imagine that Billy could respond by imitating his father's drive toward dominance over people and environment, and by pretending to understand the infinite void in his mother's life. He cannot do either, apparently, without violating his own nature. He makes a tragic compromise, which at least permits survival. He yields to his father's attitude without adopting them as a model. He withdraws from his mother without complaint, without actively hurting her. He feels, apparently, it is better to turn the other cheek than to share the guilt of any kind of aggression. Billy becomes a Jesus-figure, as we have shown in our "Textual Analysis." His very name indicates he is on a spiritual quest. His pilgrimage ironically turns for a time into a Children's Crusade: he joins the others being led off to death or captivity. He is now a chaplain's assistant, self-crucified in the corner-brace of a boxcar. The people he must now reckon with include many who took the other path. The English colonel, Derby, Lazzaro, Weary, the bombardiers who fire Dresden are all representatives of his father's world: each of them stands for some form of dominance or aggression or retaliation. Billy stands for pacifism and tolerance. In such an environment he can only appear to be a clown.

The Dresden bombing intensifies the damage to his personality. He can survive now only by denying his experiences at Dresden - we can well imagine what it was like to walk across a molten city strewn with bodies reduced to the size of logs - and he divides himself into a social half that says yes and a private half that says no. This is symbolized in his surrender to the world of Lionel Merble, who sets him up in business and marriage. Billy's ego goes along. His id rebels, first with a breakdown, then with escape into fantasy. Publicly he agrees with the Marine major who wants more bombing, more Green Berets. Privately Billy answers with two fantasies: he sees a war-film backward (which we interpret to mean that he would undo the effects of all bombing, even the effects of all resistance to bombing) and he imagines the rest of the world Balkanizing his country as a threat to peace. The paradox of modern technology - that it creates things that can crush its user - just about completes the fragmentation of Billy's soul; he cannot face even the present now, he can no longer function professionally.

But positive influences have also been at work on Billy, and he interacts for his own betterment. It is in this self-therapy that he develops as a character, and it is this development that most critics have strangely overlooked. Through Eliot Rosewater, who is also looking for alternatives to the harsh Father World, Billy is introduced to science-fiction which gives him perspective and consolation. On his own initiative, he seeks out the man who can do him the most good: the creator of *The Gutless Wonder*, a new Gospel about Jesus, and Tralfamadore. Kilgore Trout's candid presence gives Billy the strength, for the first time in eighteen years, to face what happened on February 13, 1945.

He is committed now to trying to improve not people's physical sight but their spiritual vision. We infer that this will result only in his being committed.

Vonnegut's artistry in shaping his central character is manifest in the way he has carefully used a score of secondary characters to interact meaningfully with Billy, while subtly characterizing Billy from the inside as well. Note that Billy is two different persons in military and civilian life: in the Army he is numb, confused, totally stultified; in civilian circumstances he is more expansive, more exploratory, even showing a conscious flair for a quiet **irony**. His fantasy life involves a brilliant use of symbolic situation (as with the film run backward) to speculate on the major problems of our time.

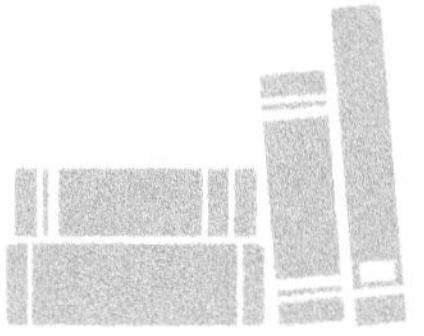

SLAUGHTERHOUSE-FIVE

CRITICS RESPOND TO SLAUGHTERHOUSE-FIVE

Publication of *Slaughterhouse-Five* precipitated two successive waves of criticism. Appearance of the novel in March 1969 was treated as a major event by *Time, Newsweek, Saturday Review, Life,* and *New York Times Book Review.* Even those critics who felt strong reservations about the literary value of Vonnegut's work were forced for the first time to take him seriously. By 1970, increasing popularity of *Slaughterhouse-Five* called for re-issue of the early novels. This set off a second big wave of criticism: *New Republic, Saturday Review, Commonweal* and other organs seized the occasion for evaluation of Vonnegut's complete works. For the first time, the first five novels were widely discussed in the national media, both for their individual merit and as progenitors of *Slaughterhouse-Five.*

SHEED: "SPLENDID ART"

One of the first to acclaim *Slaughterhouse-Five* was Wilfrid Sheed, prominent critic and himself a novelist. He opened his full-page review in *Life* (March 21, 1969) by stressing the "moral squalor" of the allied bombing of the open city of Dresden, "the greatest atrocity ever committed by Americans." Implicitly, Sheed was commending Vonnegut for being able to force the nation at long last to face the enormity of the crime. Explicitly, Sheed was explaining why Vonnegut could not write realistically about the raid - he "has written a parable instead" -and why Vonnegut's main character is a mere vegetable. For "how does the human soul recover" from the massive atrocities of our time?

> ... Billy Pilgrim represents the kind of pilgrim we are down to by this century ... on his way from Dresden to whatever heaven you can still believe in after Dresden... . Billy is not even the universal victim, who testifies to the human spirit, because his spirit is long since broken... . He is not even a "character" anymore: a pilgrim of the period was moved along by someone else's boot, so did not need to be.

Pilgrim's solution, Sheed says, is to invent a heaven "out of 20th century materials, where Good Technology triumphs over Bad Technology. His Scripture is Science Fiction, man's last good fantasy." This involved some delicate juggling of time-sequences- "a character remembering a past in which he foresees the future" - but Sheed credits Vonnegut with handling the technical difficulties with "splendid art and simplicity." Sheed recognizes, just in passing, only one shortcoming in the work when he refers to the introduction as "curiously mannered." Other critics, as we shall see, also boggle at the opening section.

HICKS: "WONDERFUL BOOK"

In his regular column in *Saturday Review*, Granville Hicks praised the "wisdom of the strategy" that Vonnegut adopted in telling his story by "indirection" (March 29, 1969). Hicks compared Vonnegut's public performance as a lecturer with his style in this "wonderful book" and concludes that "he lives and breathes in the book, and that is one reason why it is the best he has written."

SCHOLES: "EXTRAORDINARY SUCCESS"

In his page-one essay in the *New York Times Book Review* (April 6, 1969), Robert Scholes, author of *The Fabulators,* praised both Vonnegut's **theme** and his style and went on to ridicule critics who have been slow to accept Vonnegut as the "true artist" he really is. Vonnegut is to be credited, Scholes says, for stressing the fact that the unholiest deeds are done in the name of great causes. Revolution, war, crusades - these are all "ways of justifying human cruelty." Vonnegut achieves his "extraordinary success" through his humor, which is "what enables us to contemplate the horror ... he finds in contemporary existence." Vonnegut's comic style, as Scholes sees it, "reduces large areas of experience to the dimensions of a laboratory slide." He suggests we consider how much Vonnegut has managed to encompass in this brief paragraph:

Billy ... saw in his memory ... poor old Edgar Derby in front of a firing squad in the ruins of Dresden. There were only four men in that squad. Billy had heard that one man in each squad was customarily given a rifle loaded with a blank cartridge. Billy didn't think there would be a blank cartridge issued in a squad that small, in a war that old.

"The simple-minded thought processes of Billy Pilgrim are reflected in those ultra-simple sentences," Scholes notes. "But the wisdom and the verbal skill of the author shaped the final, telling phrases: 'in a squad that small, in a war that old.'"

"Serious critics," Scholes recalls, embarking now on some **irony** of his own, "have shown some reluctance to acknowledge that Vonnegut is among the best writers of his generation. He is, I suspect, both too funny and too intelligent for many, who confuse muddled earnestness with profundity."

ROWLEY: "ADMIRABLE"

Writing for Nation (June 9, 1969), Peter Rowley found *Slaughterhouse-Five* "admirable proof that the novel is not dead but... developing in technique and imaginative skill." Like Joseph Heller, Vonnegut "has extended the scope of the novel beyond the reportorial into the more imaginative," he has "found the right balance between the abstract novel," as exemplified by William Burroughs' *Nova Express*, and "realistic or 'old-school' fiction." Dresden, Rowley notes, was largely forgotten and "what an **irony** that a work of unreality should alert us to the reality of those 135,000 deaths." Rowley could find only one flaw, "a slightly disconcerting coyness at the beginning".

CAIN: "GREAT RICHES"

Seymour Cain implicitly compared Vonnegut with Voltaire and Hasek in a warm review in *Christian Century* (August 13, 1969). "Billy is ... sweet, naive, optimistic; [he] belongs to a long ... line of schlemiels, fools, and naifs. [He] is a pen-and-ink brother of Candide and Schweik and other wonderful guys." Cain stresses the very human contradictions that Vonnegut finds himself in. Almost the main message in Vonnegut, as Cain reads him, is the need "to concentrate our attention on the good moments, to summon them up from the past or the future, to strive for the state of mind where it may be said, 'Everything was beautiful and nothing hurt.' But obviously this flight through positive thinking is an unrealized dream" for Vonnegut himself, Cain says, because "he too has followed the human - not the Tralfamadorian, supra-mundane- impulse, and has taken the chance of being turned into a pillar of salt by looking back at ... Dresden." Furthermore, while Billy has learned on Tralfamadore (what Vonnegut says he learned in the University of Chicago anthropology department): that there are no villains, Vonnegut nevertheless advises his sons not to work for companies that make "massacre machinery" and to "express contempt for people who think we need machinery like that." Cain himself advises his readers to enjoy the novel "in one sitting, to hold the times together. You will find great riches in this finely wrought piece."

For the first five critics we have sampled, Vonnegut could do almost no wrong. Now let us consider the arguments of six or seven reviewers who had serious adverse criticisms of *Slaughterhouse-Five*.

STERN: "DISAPPOINTED"

In an essay in *Book World* (April 13, 1969), Daniel Stern complained that Vonnegut has indulged "in the kind of sarcastic, easily bitter philosophizing that is so obviously on the 'right side,' so sentimentally liberal, that after being amused, charmed, and impressed, ... this reader ... was disappointed and depressed." Vonnegut "is preaching. And he is too good for that." Stern found the scenes with the British prisoners of war "marvelously comic"; he admired Vonnegut's "control in the war scenes" and the "understated bitterness with which he handles the American soldiers." In short, "when Vonnegut stops preaching and is funny, I take him very seriously."

CRICHTON: "OFFENSIVE WRITER"

Also reporting mixed reactions to *Slaughterhouse-Five*, J. Michael Crichton devoted half of a long review in *New Republic* (April 26, 1969) to discussion of the changing reputation of "pulp" (western, detective, science-fiction) writers. On the credit side of the ledger he finds Vonnegut is "one of the few writers able to lift the lid off the garbage can and dispassionately examine the contents." *Slaughterhouse-Five* he describes as a "collection of impressions" each told with "the kind of economy one associates with poetry ... beautifully done, fluid, smooth and powerful." But Crichton notes that Vonnegut's style - "effortless, naive, childlike" - can be lost on anyone who has never tried to write that way. And definitely on the debit side is Vonnegut's refusal "to say who is wrong... . He becomes an offensive writer, because he will not choose sides," not ascribe "blame and penalty," not "identify good guys and bad." While it could be said that Crichton is trying to explain why Vonnegut affects some people negatively, his tone seems to imply that he has himself been affected that way.

LARDNER: "DISINGENUOUS, FATUOUS"

Almost everything good that Susan Lardner could find in the novel (New Yorker, May 17, 1969) was outweighed by something bad. To her, it is the very "vibrant simplicity of the book" which makes Vonnegut's introduction seem "disingenuous" and "objectionable." Vonnegut uses "so it goes" very shrewdly, but the "insanity of the phrase" impresses her more. "The short, flat sentences of which the novel is composed," she says, "convey shock and despair better than an array of facts or effusive mourning. Still, deliberate simplicity is as hazardous as the grand style, and Vonnegut occasionally skids into fatuousness ..." (italics supplied). Ms.

Lardner herself carefully avoids the hazards of both simplicity and the grand style by using a paragraph of Hemingway against a paragraph of Vonnegut to show how "fatuous" the latter can be.

COFFEY: "AFTER THE SEAL ACT ..."

Warren Coffey's attitude toward Vonnegut can best be described as loving despair. To him *Slaughterhouse-Five* seems further proof that Vonnegut is a promising boy who just will not work hard enough to become a responsible man (*Commonwealth*, June 6, 1969). His talent is clear in that he is a "better writer - more intelligent, more disciplined" than Joseph Heller, even. Indeed, Vonnegut is a "writer's writer, serious, technically accomplished." But his virtuosity is apparently lacking in profundity, or daring, or something. "After the seal act, bring on the lyric tenor. Something like that seems to be the formula," Coffey muses.

Romantic **irony** it used to be called - "baths of irony, followed by baths of sentiment" - and it brings in the humorist. Mr. Vonnegut seems bent on being loved not only as Class Cut-Up - that would explain the relentless intimations about how much time he used to spend looking up teacher's dress - but also as Most Sensitive Boy of 1922 - that would explain the frequent feyness. He is an inventive, skillful author working in a bad line, humor, in a bad district, Lovable Street. I admire his books, this side Westminster Abbey, but they would gain, I think, by trying something more against the grain of 1969 and their author's temperament.

But Mr. Coffey, we feel impelled to ask - what can an author do if his temperament has helped create the "grain" of our time?

Presumably, after so disposing of *Slaughterhouse-Five*, Coffey nostalgically returns to God Bless You, Mr. Rosewater, which he considers "much the best" of Vonnegut's eight books. (At least Coffey gives ample evidence that he's read the earlier works that he refers to. Ms. Lardner, however, seems not to have looked beyond the titles, thus confusing short-story collections with novels, for she opens her review by calling *Slaughterhouse-Five* "his seventh novel.")

RICHARDSON: "INFANTILE STOICISM"

If Coffey's review smacks of loving despair, Jack Richardson's bristles with savage scorn (*New York Review of Books*, July 2, 1970). First Richardson measures Vonnegut against certain predecessors whom Vonnegut should take as his models. Jonathan Swift was tops as a "social fantast" and Samuel Butler was somewhat less great; G. B. Shaw was good but inferior to Butler and George Orwell barely made it. These four satirists "provide a neat descending scale of fantast ability which anticipates the arrival and style of a writer like Vonnegut." As a matter of fact, "he so badly abuses the tradition of deft argument which his predecessors have established that one wonders whether they didn't anticipate him as a character rather than as a fellow writer." Richardson hurls epithet after epithet at Vonnegut: "soft, sentimental satirist," "popularizer of easy whimsy," "compiler of easy-to-read truisms." His ideas are "facile and fleshy," his writing is "flat and graceless," "unsurprising, self-indulgent," "taking no pains to disguise how pleased it is with itself," characterized by "wearisome uninventiveness" and "infantile stoicism." Vonnegut is guilty of "destruction of fine distinctions and the substitution of blurred, flaccid fault-finding for critical rage." He just does not know "how carefully balanced a book must be that wishes to encompass the annihilation of millions and the mental caprices of one dull hero."

Reading Richardson's tirade, we wonder, if Vonnegut is really that trivial, why does it take more than 2,000 words of carefully smelted invective to dispose of him? We imagine Richardson as huffing and puffing for 500 words and then, noting that Vonnegut is still there, huffing and puffing another 500 and so on. And isn't there something unbelievable about that "neat descending scale"? About arranging the entire history of a literary **genre** to prove that your enemy occupies the low point in the decline and fall? The word "enemy" slips out, but it is the only word to describe Richardson's target. What else but one's personal enemy could call forth such hostility? Trigger off such "overkill"? What seems to enrage Richardson most (aside from the fact that he is mysteriously threatened by Vonnegut) is Vonnegut's failure to express rage. Social fantasts of the past have fueled their arguments with manly rage (Richardson grades them according to their savagery) and Vonnegut is a traitor for not following tradition. This is a poor demonstration of "deft argument." It shows too that Richardson has not even listened to Vonnegut's argument. And so he has missed a major point that Scholes, for example, in his calmer review, did not miss when he emphasized that evil deeds are done in the name of great causes, and crusades are "ways of justifying human cruelty." Richardson seems engaged in a great crusade, a great cause. But Vonnegut is interested in demonstrating that the evil is in all of us and he has grown beyond rage, beyond looking for the evil in them or in him. Vonnegut and his admirers are weary and wary of self-righteous rage because it blinds one to the evil in oneself. To a typical Vonnegutian, Richardson's chest-thumping overkill rage is ludicrous, as "comical" as the antics of the home-coming "hero" in *Happy Birthday, Wanda June*.

TODD "CRUELEST CASE"

Nevertheless, Richardson did raise at least one valid question, one that was further discussed by Richard Todd in a long and sensitive study of Vonnegut (*New York Times Magazine*, January 24, 1971). "One critic," Todd says, "was angered that all of Vonnegut's social ideas are not shocking but banal.... Richardson wrote ... that 'Vonnegut is a moralist too easily satisfied that the world confirms his ... view. ... He stops where an intelligent imagination ought to begin.'"

"This," Todd says, "is the cruelest case that can be put against Vonnegut's work ... it seems certain that ... Richardson has identified a problem with Vonnegut as social satirist. Vonnegut is attacking an America that has already been laid waste by such writers as Sinclair Lewis and H. L. Mencken... . It is not that American vulgarity, greed, militarism, obsession with machines have perished, only that they are shot-up targets for an artist, and hard to render freshly."

Both Todd and Richardson fail to note that while satirists like Lewis and Mencken did the job to the satisfaction of the older generation, they have not done the job required by the younger generation. Lewis and Mencken were, by comparison with Vonnegut, negative writers, critics of the *Establishment* who offered no alternative position. Vonnegut, on the other hand, offers what Schickel called, as early as 1966, "a unique vision," a program for dissidents.

KAZIN: "A BOY'S FANTASY"

Two of Vonnegut's techniques in *Slaughterhouse-Five* - his science-fiction and his "strategy of indirection" - are totally wasted on Alfred Kazin ("The War Novel: From Mailer to Vonnegut," Saturday Review, February 6, 1971). "Vonnegut's use of space fiction," Kazin says, "is always too droll for my taste, a boy's fantasy of more rational creatures than ourselves." Kazin seems to shake his head in dismay at Vonnegut's failure to "protest" or even "explain" the Dresden raid. At first Kazin doesn't judge Vonnegut too severely for this because "he seems, all too understandably, subdued by his material and plays it dumb." As a consequence, however, the "book is short, loose, and somehow helpless." But when Kazin compares Vonnegut's treatment with another writer's he becomes much sterner in his tone.

"In his remarkable account of being cooped up in Germany, *Castle to Castle*, [Louis-Ferdinand] Celine, on the basis of information given him by the Vichy consul in Dresden, tells us more what the Dresden fire-bombing was like than does Vonnegut, who was there." Kazin offers samples from Celine:

... the tactic of total squashing and frying in phosphorus ... American invention really perfected the last "new look" before the A-bomb ... first the suburbs, the periphery, with liquid sulfur and avalanches of torpedoes ... then general roasting ... the whole center! Act II ... churches, parks, museums ... no survivors wanted...

"Why," Kazin asks, "does the American who was there avoid such strong, plain language? Celine's bluntness, his graphic power, incorporates his willingness to take sides, his deep political outrage at the specific American 'tactic of total squashing and frying in phosphorus.' Vonnegut's evasion of any realistic description seems typical of the purely moral, unpolitical, widespread American sense of futility about our government's having made war in and on Indochina for an entire decade."

Kazin seems here indifferent to the fact that Vonnegut's main concern is not with the immediate sensations of the Dresden raid but with its long-range effects on the Billy Pilgrims of the world. Kazin does not acknowledge Vonnegut's message, part of which is that moral outrage over the raid would resemble the self-righteousness that made the raid possible in the first place. But in linking Vonnegut's attitude to Dresden with popular attitudes to Vietnam, Kazin is certainly on the right track.

REISSUE OF EARLIER WORKS

Time was ripe for reissue of Vonnegut's other five novels, some of which had been out of print for years. And so in 1970 Vonnegut enjoyed unusual privilege and prestige: he had all of his novels in print at the same time, in both hard-cover and paperback. And this gave the critics the perfect opportunity for in-depth appraisal of the works of Vonnegut, their overall meaning and their contribution to literary art.

RANLY: "FIVE VONNEGUT PARLOR GAMES"

Father Ernest W. Ranly ingeniously structures his essay ("What Are People For?" Commonweal, May 7, 1971) by outlining five "parlor games" that "Vonnegut people" play. These are (1) personal biography: object is to match Vonnegut's fictional persons, places, and things with real people and events in the author's life; Ilium Works, e.g., is General Electric, Vonnegut's ex-employer; (2) reappearance: object is to trace the recurrence of Vonnegut's places, characters, objects in different stories; e.g., Pilgrim's Tralfamadore first figured in *The Sirens of Titan*; (3) style: object is to discuss the function and value of Vonnegut's various techniques; Ranly credits Willis E. McNelly for playing this game brilliantly in an America article in which he equates Vonnegut's use of science fiction with T. S. Eliot's "objective correlative" which enables us "to face problems we cannot otherwise face directly." McNelly, Ranly says, "understands that Vonnegut cannot (nor can any human) face directly evils so incomprehensible as the fire-bombing of Dresden.... Vonnegut employs science fiction as a ploy to give him distance and objectivity ... in order to retell the horror"; (4) Vonnegut's meaning: object is to determine just what it is that Vonnegut is trying to say; this game provides Ranly with his chance to review all the themes, explicit and implicit, in all six novels and selected short stories, and leads him to the game he is himself most interested in: (5) criticism of Vonnegut's thought.

As Ranly reads him, Vonnegut conceives of an utterly indifferent God in control of the universe, with his "prize creature," man, so built he thinks he must be able to discover a purpose for himself. Ranly draws a parallel to Beckett: Vonnegut sees man as waiting for Godot who will never come. How, asks Ranly, does one respond to Vonnegut?

"The primary issue is the very meaning of purpose and design ... in spite of himself (and maybe because of his expertise in science fiction), Vonnegut seems caught up in the intellectual presuppositions of science and does not seem able to extricate himself."

For mechanistic science, Ranly says, purpose means controlled design, antecedents and consequents, directed toward a finished product. But in talking about purpose of the universe, we must mean something much wider, more profound than this "narrow notion" of mechanistic design. God may have made the universe good but not necessarily "functional" in a mechanistic sense. "That the universe is made ... with compassion, made beautiful, and in fun (out of pure whimsy) may be wonderfully real reasons for its existence, unsatisfying reasons for a modern scientist."

He concludes that it is because "Vonnegut employs only a scientific, mechanistic meaning for purpose" that he "fails to find a reasonable purpose in either the universe or in man... . Vonnegut is correct when he wants man to have the freedom to be undependable, inefficient, unpredictable and non-durable." Vonnegut is correct too to rail against science's reification of man. "Now let Vonnegut tell a human story in which people fall in love and have a non-mechanized history (not even manipulated by the Tralfamadoreans). What in hell are people for? To fall in love, be happy, enjoy beauty, ... discover joy. Yes, there will be human failings, unfaithfulness, inconsistency, but that, again, is man's story."

How does one make a response to Ranly? Well, Vonnegut has written such stories, and some of them are reprinted in *Welcome to the Monkey House* ("Long Walk to Forever," for example). And we could say that when the Shah raised the question "What are people for?" (*Player Piano*), he was really asking a rhetorical question. He was really saying, why automate everything when that deprives people of a sense of personal contribution and worth? Are we here to prove the infallibility of machines or to give men a chance to function and express themselves? And we could say, finally, that Professor Ranly has only a lover's quarrel with Vonnegut: it is obvious they really disagree on only small details. Ranly's essay has served as one of the best short introductions to Vonnegut in print.

DE MOTT: "GOOD BREAK FOR THE AGE"

Novelist and critic Benjamin De Mott took the occasion of Vonnegut's novels being "back in print" to consider the question, "What is Vonnegut's charm for the young?" First he considers the possibility that Vonnegut provides "escape from dailiness." For a "free-form universe of discourse-fantasy-sermon-satire-can function as a kind of alternative community, a refuge from the oppressive rule of things as they are." But this, De Mott decided, is only one element in Vonnegut's success. "The case is that Vonnegut is [also] loved for ... a congeries of opinions, prejudices, and assumptions perfectly tuned to the mind of the emergent generation."

The main beliefs of the "Youthcult," with which Vonnegut perfectly harmonizes, are, according to De Mott:

1. people in power are hung up on procedures and formalities, blind to the great issues, scared of facing the facts

2. the world is on the verge of disaster

3. the work ethic "begets and is begotten by" cruelty and hatred

4. attempts of the Establishment to hide prevailing brutality are criminal and doomed to failure

5. open-mindedness is the highest virtue; the root of our troubles is a moral and intellectual rigidity, a belief in absolutes

6. man must transcend the Ego, penetrate to states of consciousness where time sequence breaks down and time periods coexist

DeMott cites passages in Vonnegut's work that corroborate or parallel each of these "dogmas."

His review of Vonnegut's oeuvre convinces De Mott that the "strongest writing ... is found in the least fanciful, most tightly made tales," *Player Piano* and *Mother Night*. Here De Mott finds that the comedy "cuts cleanest when the subject in view is that of classical satire-self-delusion," Otherwise, Vonnegut's work can be "lax, rambling, ... sad-eyed, sticky," often "formless, incoherent, a mix of joke book tunes, fantasies, cartoon and sermonical Luddite posturings, outcries against cruelty and greed." But, says De Mott, "viciousness has no dominion" over Vonnegut, who "may dream of black comedy" while "kindness keeps breaking in ..."

Viewed esthetically, then, the results aren't "uniformly exhilarating" to De Mott, for "art and intellect vanish periodically" and "bull-session simplisms often mound up and drift." Nevertheless, De Mott cautions, there are times in the history of letters when the "nature of a writer's best or worst self in literary terms matters less than the function the man performs for his primary audience." And Vonnegut's work, he finds, "does serve a function. Its unbrutal laughter is a surcease from high-fashion meanness and knowingness." De Mott concludes that "on balance, the kids' lighting on Kurt Vonnegut is an undeservedly good break for the age."

SAMUELS: "ADOLESCENT RIDICULE"

Going over the same ground, Charles Thomas Samuels ("Age of Vonnegut," *New Republic*, June 12, 1971) turns De Mott's emphasis inside out and uses Vonnegut's success as condemnation of our times. "... we can't yet know what Vonnegut has done for his youthful constituency," Samuels replies to De Mott, but "his books, at this very moment, tell us what he has done for literature."

Samuels deduces that Vonnegut is a "bogus talent" whose books are "littered with the stale fruit of received wisdom" and "uninventive to the point of repetition." In Vonnegut, alas, the fine art of **satire** is "reduced to mockery of invented targets." Worst of all, Vonnegut appeals to those who already believe what he has to say; "this saves the artist from the terrible bother of art." And Samuels doesn't find it difficult to see why Vonnegut appeals to youngsters.

His own spiritual age is late adolescence: the time when a flip manner often disguises priggishness, when skepticism is just a hedge against vulnerability, when prejudice disdains the search for proof and inexperience limits one's power to imagine, when confidence in one's special distinction reveals itself in the very fervor with which it is denied and the herding instinct asserts a need for independence.

Samuels acknowledges that it's "disconcerting" that Vonnegut is also "beloved by critics (and presumably adult readers)."

For them, he provides an easy bridge from an age of skepticism and baffled hope to one of faith in any nostrum that bears the certifications of youth.

Samuels concludes that Vonnegut is important not in his effect but as a symptom. He can tell us nothing worth knowing except what his rise itself indicates: ours is an age in which adolescent ridicule can become a mode of upward mobility.

TANNER: "MOVING MEDITATION"

Several critics, as we have seen, ridicule Vonnegut for being "banal" in his thought and for offering "stale fruit of received wisdom." Just how superficially, tendentiously, and impatiently these critics have examined Vonnegut is made clear by more ambitious, more profound studies in which the implicit meanings of Vonnegut's work are recognized. Best of these to date is the chapter on Vonnegut in the British critic Tony Tanner's superb book, *City of Words: American Fiction 1950–1970.* Tanner examines all six Vonnegut novels in detail to ascertain what they reveal about the American temperament and about the author's original contributions in **theme** and style.

Tanner finds four **themes** in Vonnegut that he calls characteristically American: (1) the "desire for some sort of flexible form which we can find in so many American novels"; (2) a "suspicion of all communication that seems to go so deep in contemporary American fiction"; (3) "opposition between the fixed and the flowing" which is "very common in contemporary American fiction"; and (4) the "typical American " desire for "a place beyond all plots and systems, some private space, or 'border area,' - a house by the side of the road of history."

Tanner finds Vonnegut strongly original in exploring these main questions: (1) "What is the relationship between the facts we encounter and the fictions we invent?" Given, for example, "the terrible historical actuality of the Second World War, what are we to make of the ambiguous role of fantasy in men's lives?" (2) What is "man's status as agent-victim"? Several Vonnegut heroes think of themselves as free agents but they (and/or we) realize they are really being used: we are treated to the "spectacle of the plotter plotted." A basic dilemma in Vonnegut's work, says Tanner, is that both sides want to "impose a role" on a hero, make him part of "someone else's plan." (3) What is the relationship between patterns of reality? "Every pattern may in fact be part of a larger pattern outside its control." Corollaries: What is the relation between the "surface message and the hidden content?" between the parts of the self?

Tanner's critical comments on each of the novels are fresh and provocative. We infer that he considers *Cat's Cradle* the best of the earlier works ("brilliant little fiction") and there is no doubt that he views *Slaughterhouse-Five* as Vonnegut's magnum opus. This "masterly novel ... seems almost to summarize and conclude the sequence of his previous five novels"; it is "a moving meditation on the relationship between history and dreaming, cast in an appropriately factual/fictional mode... . The facts which defy explanation are brought into the same frame with fictions beyond verification." Tanner explicitly draws our attention to the possibility that Vonnegut has been influenced by Hesse; and although he does not specify it, by his very formulation of Vonnegut's **themes** Tanner leads us to perceive some similar relation between Vonnegut and Beckett.

In his overall judgment of Vonnegut, Tanner recognizes both strengths and weaknesses:

The distinctive tone is very likeable and sympathetic; it bespeaks a compassionate humane spirit. The economy and laconic wit prevent this from issuing in much overt sentimentality, though the tendency is there ... at times it does seem as though he is using fiction to issue short sermons ... and this can endanger the poise of the work ...

What Vonnegut has accomplished, says Tanner, is to "define with clarity and economy - and compassion - the nature and composition of [man's] confusion."

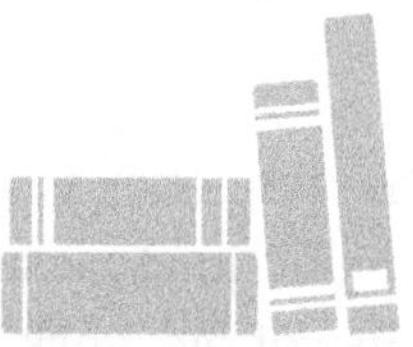

BIBLIOGRAPHY

EDITIONS OF VONNEGUT'S WORKS

Player Piano

New York: Charles Scribner's, 1952.

London: Macmillan, 1953.

New York: Holt, Rinehart and Winston, 1966.

New York: Avon (paperback), 1967. New edition (Bard/Avon), 1970.

New York: Seymour Lawrence/Delacorte, 1970.

The Sirens of Titan

New York: Houghton Mifflin, 1959.

London: Gollancz, 1962.

New York: Dell (paperback), 1967. New edition, 1970.

New York: Seymour Lawrence/Delacorte, 1970.

Canary in a Cathouse

New York: Gold Medal (paperback), 1961.

Mother Night

New York: Gold Medal (paperback), 1961.

New York: Harper and Row, 1966.

New York: Avon (paperback), 1967. New edition (Bard/Avon), 1970.

London: Jonathan Cape, 1968.

New York: Seymour Lawrence/Delacorte, 1970.

Cat's Cradle

New York: Holt, Rinehart and Winston, 1963.

New York: Dell (paperback), 1963. New edition, 1970.

London: Gollancz, 1963.

New York: Seymour Lawrence/Delacorte, 1971.

God Bless You, Mr. Rosewater; or *Pearls Before Swine*

New York: Holt, Rinehart and Winston, 1965. London: Jonathan Cape, 1965. New York: Dell (paperback), 1965. New edition, 1970. New York: Seymour Lawrence/Delacorte, 1970.

Welcome to the Monkey House

New York: Delacorte, 1968.

New York: Dell (paperback), 1970.

Slaughterhouse-Five; or, *The Children's Crusade; A Duty-Dance with Death*

New York: Seymour Lawrence/Delacorte, 1969.

London: Jonathan Cape, 1970.

New York: Dell (paperback), 1970.

Happy Birthday, Wanda June; a play

New York: Seymour Lawrence/Delacorte, 1971.

Between Time and Timbuktu

New York: Seymour Lawrence/Delacorte, 1972.

New York: Delta (paperback), 1972.

Selected Writings About Vonnegut And His Works

Bryan, C. D. B. "Kurt Vonnegut, Head Bokononist." *New York Times Book Review*, April 6, 1969, pp. 2, 25. Sketch of Vonnegut and a survey of the Vonnegut canon published on the day the Sunday Times carried Scholes' review of *Slaughterhouse-Five*. Bryan describes Vonnegut as "an amiable Cassandra" whose two main messages are: "Be Kind" and "God doesn't care whether you are or not."

Cain, Seymour. "Pillar of Salt." *Christian Century* 86 (August 13, 1969), pp. 1069–1070. Sensitive, sympathetic interpretation, with insightful comments on Vonnegut's **themes** and techniques; especially good on his use of the naif and the meaning of the **allusion** to Lot's wife.

Christian Century. "Banning of Billy Pilgrim." 88 (June 2, 1971), p. 681. Editorial regret over Judge Arthur Moore's banning of *Slaughterhouse-Five* from Rochester High School in Oakland County, Michigan, in May 1971. "... there are obscenities ... in *Slaughterhouse-Five*, but none so great ... to match the obscenity of the Dresden raid itself ... or the self-righteousness of Moore's judicial interference in the selection of literature for school use."

Coffey, Warren. "Gentleness and a stylish sense of the ridiculous." *Commonweal* 90 (June 6, 1969), pp. 347–348. Obviously a faithful Vonnegut reader, Coffey nevertheless regards *Slaughterhouse-Five* as just "another single" by an author who could hit home-runs more regularly (if he'd imbibe more Coffey).

Contemporary Authors. "Vonnegut, Kurt, Jr." Volumes 1–4 (first revision). Detroit, Mich.: Gale Research, 1967. Excellent perspective on Vonnegut's position in American literature in 1967, when *Slaughterhouse-Five* was listed as "work in progress."

Crichton, J. Michael. "Sci-Fi and Vonnegut." *New Republic* 160 (April 2, 1969), pp. 33–35. Review of literary status of science-fiction, leading to survey of Vonnegut's own reputation, first as "sci-fi" writer, then as black humorist, then as "serious author." Interesting comments on left-wingers' (alleged) reactions to *Mother Night* and on *Cat's Cradle* as book in which Vonnegut developed techniques suitable for *Slaughterhouse-Five*.

Current Biography Yearbook 1970. "Vonnegut, Kurt, Jr." Pp. 429–432. Also in Current Biography 31 (July 1970), pp. 43–46. Compact synthesis of information available in newspaper and magazine accounts, including quotations from critics and from statements Vonnegut has made in major interviews.

DeMott, Benjamin. "Vonnegut's Otherworldly Laughter." *Saturday Review* 54 (May 1, 1971), pp. 29–32, 38. DeMott seizes the occasion of the reissue of Vonnegut's first five novels to conduct a "sober inquiry" into reasons for Vonnegut's "authority" among the young. DeMott concludes that the main reason is that Vonnegut's values are "perfectly tuned" to the mind of "youthcult," and that although Vonnegut isn't consistently artistic or even intellectual, his appeal to the youth is a "good break" for our time.

Hicks, Granville. "Literary Horizons." *Saturday Review* 52 (March 29, 1969), p. 25. Hicks considers Vonnegut a "humorist and satirist in the vein of Mark Twain and Jonathan Swift" and calls *Slaughterhouse-Five* the "best he has written."

Johnston, A. "Authors and Editors." *Publisher's Weekly* 195 (April 21, 1969), pp. 20–21.

Kazin, Alfred. "The War Novel: From Mailer to Vonnegut." *Saturday Review* 54 (February 6, 1971), pp. 13–15, 36. Essentially, Kazin echoes the old complaints about Vonnegut: his space fiction is "a boy's fantasy about creatures more rational than ourselves" and his handling of the Dresden fire-bombing is inferior to Louis-Ferdinand Celine's (in *Castle to Castle*) because Celine is willing "to take sides" and Vonnegut isn't.

Lardner, Susan. "Books: Dresden and Dunedin." *New Yorker* 45 (May 17, 1969), pp. 145–146. Ms. Lardner reacts queasily to Vonnegut's "exchanging feeling for outerspatial detachment"; she compares Vonnegut's "deliberate simplicity" with Hemingway's to prove that the Master never and Vonnegut sometimes "skids into fatuousness."

Menken, Nancy. Review of *Slaughterhouse-Five. Library Journal* 94 (December 15, 1969), p. 4624.

Newsweek. "46 - And Trusted." 73 (March 3, 1969), p. 79. Survey of Vonnegut's popularity, as writer and lecturer, on the eve of publication of *Slaughterhouse-Five*.

O'Connell, Shaun. Review of *Slaughterhouse-Five*. American Scholar 38 (Autumn 1969), p. 718.

Ranly, Ernest W. "What are People For? Man, Fate, and Kurt Vonnegut." *Commonweal* 94 (May 7, 1971), pp. 207–210. Excellent discussion of Vonnegut's **themes** and message by a priest and philosophy professor who writes with unpretentious directness and relevance.

Reed, John. Review of *Slaughterhouse-Five. Christian Science Monitor*, April 17, 1969, p. 15.

Richardson, Jack. "Easy Writer." *New York Review of Books*, July 2, 1970, pp. 7–8. Furious, seemingly motiveless assault on Vonnegut, whom Richardson pictures as time-serving, facile, and obvious in his conclusions; blowzy, flaccid, and slapdash in style; smug in his tone; utterly unable to create a character, reflect the intricacies or real life, or spin a compelling yarn. To Richardson, the art of social fantasy reached its apotheosis in Jonathan Swift, declined with Butler and Shaw, was barely kept alive by Orwell, and has died in Vonnegut.

Robinson, W. C. *Review. Library Journal* 94 (March 1, 1969), p. 1021.

Rowley, Peter. "So it Goes." *Nation* 208 (June 9, 1969), pp. 736–737. Hails Vonnegut because -like Heller - he is extending the scope of the novel "beyond the reportorial into the more imaginative."

Samuels, Charles Thomas. "Age of Vonnegut." *New Republic* 164 (June 12, 1971), pp. 30–32. Samuels argues that Vonnegut's popularity proves "ours is an age in which adolescent ridicule can become a mode of upward mobility." While putting Vonnegut down as a "bogus talent," Samuels nevertheless offers solid descriptions of techniques of "advanced novelists in the modern period."

Schickel, Richard. "**Black Comedy** with Purifying Laughter." *Harper's* 232 (May 1966), pp. 103–106. An attempt (three years before publication of *Slaughterhouse-Five*) to "encourage serious people to take [Vonnegut] seriously." Schickel resented critics' efforts to snub Vonnegut by dubbing him first as a science-fiction writer, then as a black humorist, then as a "cult" writer. Schickel saw Vonnegut as better than any of these pejorative labels would imply: "a man with a unique vision ...[an] unimitative and inimitable social satirist" who has "advanced from diagnostician to exorcist."

Scholes, Robert. *The Fabulators*. N.Y.: *Oxford University Press*, 1967. Thoughtful argument for the values of the new non-realistic fiction as exemplified in the (up-to-1967) works of Durrell, Hawkes, Barth, Murdock, and Vonnegut. While regarding Vonnegut as an inheritor of both the picaresque and satiric traditions, Scholes demonstrates how and why Vonnegut departs from conventional **satire**. Scholes offers good definitions of **Black Humor** and makes neat distinctions between the answer offered by the Black Humorist and that offered by the existentialist.

Scholes, Robert. "Like Lot's Wife, He Looked Back - at the destruction of Dresden and 135,000 dead." *New York Times Book Review*, April 6, 1969, pp. 1, 23. Perfect tribute to the book - to its themes, implications, techniques - as well as the perfect answer to Vonnegut's most hostile critics.

Sheed, Wilfrid. "Requiem to Billy Pilgrim's Progress." *Life* 66 (March 21, 1969), p. 9. Masterful explanation of why Billy is "not even a 'character'" and why Vonnegut makes it a "book of carefully strangled emotions."

____. "The Now Generation Knew Him When." *Life* 67 (September 12, 1969), pp. 64–66, 69. Colorful, candid sketches of Vonnegut as father, soldier, villager, driver, writer, and conversationalist, by a critic who became his house-guest.

____. *The Morning After; Selected Essays and Reviews.* N.Y.: Farrar, Straus & Giroux, 1971. The section on *Slaughterhouse-Five* (pp. 276–279) is a reprint of Sheed's *Life* magazine article of March 21, 1969.

Stern, Daniel, *Review.* Book World, April 13, 1969, p. 7. Disapproves of what he sees as Vonnegut's didacticism; likes only those scenes in which Vonnegut "stops preaching."

Tanner, Tony. *City of Words: American Fiction*, 1950–1970. N.Y.: Harper & Row, 1971. Tanner's chapter on Vonnegut (pp. 181–201, "The Uncertain Messenger") comprises a sensitive, objective review and interpretation of all six of Vonnegut's novels. Tanner examines Vonnegut as one of 25 American writers engaged in re-shaping the art of fiction.

Time. "The Price of Survival." 93 (April 11, 1969), pp. 106, 108. Likens Vonnegut to the sixteenth-century mystic, Sebastian Franck; calls his attitudes "old-fashioned Populist"; credits him with 20 years of paving the way for ideas "now fashionable."

Todd, Richard. "The Masks of Kurt Vonnegut Jr." *New York Times* Magazine, January 24, 1971, pp. 16–17, 19, 22, 24, 26, 30–31. The editor of *The Atlantic* gives his acute first-hand observations of Vonnegut's semester at Harvard (Fall 1970) when he taught creative writing, gave a public lecture and reading, and held office hours for students.

Printed in the USA
CPSIA information can be obtained
at www.ICGtesting.com
LVHW011131090124
768522LV00030B/457